# 4
# Ingredients
# 2

# 4 Ingredients 2

**4 Ingredients**
**PO Box 1171**
**Mooloolaba QLD 4557**

ABN: 19 307 118 068

www.4ingredients.co.uk
info@4ingredients.co.uk

*4 Ingredients 2*

Cover & Formatting: Allure Creative, www.allurecreative.com.au

UK Distributor:      Simon & Schuster UK (020) 7316 1900
AUS Distributor:    Simon & Schuster (02) 9983 6600
NZ Distributor:      Random House (09) 444 7197

ISBN: 978-0-85720-056-3

Printed in the UK by CPI Mackays, Chatham ME5 8TD

# Foreword

WELL ... WHO WOULD EVER HAVE THOUGHT ... Two girls who met 39 years ago would not only remain friends into adulthood, but also join forces to write the biggest selling Cookbook not only in Australia but also New Zealand for 2007!!! Even more amazingly go on to write this, our second *4 Ingredients* cookbook! Every day, we are asked just how we did it. A few things you know; Kim had the idea for this cookbook before approaching Rachael who had previously self published and written a book and who had the marketing and book writing experience to make it fly. Together we pooled our talents to construct a cookbook we needed in our everyday lives ... THAT WAS THE EASY PART!

But what most people don't know is that NO publisher shared our enthusiasm and vision for what a godsend this book actually was – THIS WAS THE HARD PART!!! We tag teamed and called every publisher in Australia we could get a phone number for, and even one in New Zealand! Whilst we thought we had a winner, they thought otherwise with responses ranging from ' Are you famous?', 'Oh not another cookbook' to the classic one ' CLUNK!' Fortunately we are resilient, so we simply sought other avenues to make it happen. Kim stepped up to the plate and funded the setup and printing of the book while Rachael got busy setting up a website, business and marketing plan that would ensure that the book would sell. In the meantime, however, we still had one major challenge, and that was we didn't have any distribution channel other than OURSELVES!!!!

We called 4 distributors and all refused but one! We had the great fortune to be connected to the operations manager, Ed Petrie of Sydney based distributor Gary Allen. To his absolute credit, he listened to us and didn't hang up!!! In fact by the end of the conversation he asked us to send him a copy!!!!!!!!!!!!!! Even MORE to his credit, he accepted our draft copy as we hadn't yet printed the book!

Three long weeks of waiting were finally over when Ed called back saying that of the 10 self-published titles they see across their desks every week, they may only accept one title per month (if any!) ... Ours was one of them! YAAAYYY!!! What we didn't realise of course was that this meant all 1,000 books we sent to them were strictly on consignment basis and that we would have to wait for them to be ordered by booksellers, then wait three months before our first payday ... We had to create demand!

From there, each day when our 3 beautiful boys had a nap, we began to implement our marketing plan. We sent our press release to every radio station, newspaper, magazine and TV program in the country AND followed up each with a phone call. We also rang every bookstore in Australia, we introduced ourselves, told them about our terrific book and thanked them in advance for ANY support they could hand our way!

We organised book-signings from one end of this vast country to the other, we booked motels and hotels, flights, taxis and hire cars all at our expense. We did this all around our families daily lives and activities and knowing we had the love and support of our wonderful husbands Glen and Paul, because without them we would have been unable to travel.

We are often told that we don't realise just what we did in 2007. From our initial 2,000 we went on to print over 420,000 books for the year!!!!!!!!! And truth be told, we still don't think about the magnitude of it. All we did (and still do) is put in lots of time and work to achieve what we wanted to do in the only way we knew how ... hard work! We also had an enormous amount of good fortune along the way, such as being blessed with remarkable families and friends. We are extremely grateful to for their generosity; giving freely of their time, their love and support without which we could not have achieved all that we did!

To Ed Petrie, we single you out because you went in to bat for our book with a gut feeling it could work and for you, we are soooooo glad it did. You do what you do brilliantly and we thank you for taking a chance on us.

To the booksellers who embraced us and supported us, who kept ordering, telling people about it, and continue to do so ... We thank you very much.

To everyone who believed our story, and thought it good enough to print, to interview, to film for various audiences we thank you for helping us to spread the love ... You are sensational and we really appreciate it!

To all who sent (in particular the very generous Marie McColl) or emailed recipes through, thank you so much. The ideas you had were just too good to keep to ourselves, and it is from you the inspiration for this second book sprang! We hope sharing our story also inspires you to do whatever it is you are thinking of doing, because you never know where a good idea, a bit of motivation, and a tonne of work may lead you!!!!!

And finally, THANK YOU for being part of our journey by owning a copy of our book.

*Rachael & Kim*

# In the Cupboard

In *4 Ingredients 2* we have a suggestion of ingredients you may want to stock to help you create many a wonderful meals and treats from the pages within!

*Please note: Again, in this book we have not included salt, pepper and water as part of the 4 ingredients.*

| SAVOURY | SWEET |
|---|---|
| Basil Pesto | Arrowroot biscuits |
| bbq sauce | Caster sugar |
| Beef & chicken stock cubes | Cinnamon |
| Breadcrumbs | Condensed milk |
| Cold pressed macadamia nut oil, rice bran oil, sunflower oil | Cornflour |
| Curry powder | Cream |
| Dijon mustard | Cream cheese |
| Extra virgin macadamia oil spray | Desiccated coconut |
| French onion soup (dry mix) | Evaporated milk |
| Fresh vegetables | Food colouring |
| Garlic | Free range eggs |
| Lemons | Fresh fruit |
| Minced ginger | Gelatine |
| Peppercorns | Honey |
| Pine nuts | Icing sugar |
| Rice | Jams: Apricot, strawberry |
| Sea salt | Jelly crystals |
| Sesame seeds | Marmalade |
| Ready rolled shortcrust pastry | Mixed dried fruit |
| Spaghetti & noodles | Mixed spices |
| Sour cream | Nutmeg |
| Soy sauce | Plain & self raising flour |
| Sweet chilli sauce | Pkt. bamboo skewers |
| Tinned soups: Asparagus, Celery etc. | Pkt. vanilla cake mix |
| Tomato sauce | Ready rolled puff pastry (preferably with butter) |
| Whole-egg mayonnaise | Sugar (raw, brown) |
| Worcestershire sauce | Tinned fruit: Pineapple, pear |
| Vegetable Seasoning | Tin of pie apple |
| Vegetable Stock | Vanilla essence |
| Vinegar | |

# Guide to Weights & Measures

A big fancy conversion table is not required as all you need to make the recipes within each edition of 4 Ingredients are:

1 teaspoon (1 tsp.)
1 tablespoon (1 tbs.)
1 cup (250ml)
or the following:

| | Grams per cup | | Grams per cup |
|---|---|---|---|
| Almond Meal | 170 | Nuts - Pecans | 120 |
| BBQ Sauce | 280 | Nuts – Pine nuts | 160 |
| Butter | 230 | Nuts - Pistachios | 120 |
| Basil pesto | 260 | Nuts – Walnuts | 100 |
| Breadcrumbs | 130 | Pasta (dried) | 75 |
| Brown sugar, packed | 220 | Pasta sauce | 175 |
| Caster sugar | 200 | Peanut butter | 260 |
| Cheese | 100 | Polenta | 170 |
| Chutney | 300 | Popcorn | 40 |
| Cornflakes | 120 | Raisins | 170 |
| Cornflour | 120 | Rice | 185 |
| Desiccated coconut | 120 | Rice bubbles | 80 |
| Dried apricots | 160 | Rolled oats | 100 |
| Dried mixed fruit | 170 | Salsa | 175 |
| Dukkah | 120 | Sour Cream | 320 |
| Flour – plain | 175 | Sultanas | 170 |
| Flour – self raising | 175 | Sugar – White | 220 |
| Honey | 320 | Sugar – Raw | 200 |
| Icing Sugar | 120 | Sweet Chilli Sauce | 320 |
| Jam | 320 | Tandoori paste | 225 |
| Maple Syrup | 240 | Teriyaki sauce | 280 |
| Mayonnaise | 260 | Tomato paste | 260 |
| Natural muesli | 110 | Tomato sauce | 280 |
| Nuts - Almonds | 160 | Yoghurt | 250 |

# Abbreviations Used

| | |
|---|---|
| Gram | g |
| Kilogram | kg |
| Millilitre | ml |
| Litre | ltr |

# Oven Temperature Guide

Making friends with your oven really helps when cooking. Basically the Celsius temperature is about half the Fahrenheit temperature.

Most ovens these days offer the option to bake or fan bake (amongst others); as a rule, the fan-assisted option will greatly increase the temperature in your oven and will decrease cooking times.

**Our recipes have been compiled assuming a fan-forced oven unless otherwise stated.** If, however, your oven is conventional as a general rule of thumb fan-forced cooking temperatures are increased by 20°C (this may vary between models). So if the recipe reads 'bake for 1 hour at 200°C' that will be 1 hour at 220°C in a conventional oven.

**Here's some help:**

| | Slow | Slow | Mod | Mod | Mod hot | Mod hot | Hot | Hot | Very hot |
|---|---|---|---|---|---|---|---|---|---|
| Fahrenheit | 275 | 300 | 325 | 350 | 375 | 400 | 425 | 450 | 475 |
| Celsius | 140 | 150 | 165 | 180 | 190 | 200 | 220 | 230 | 240 |
| Gas Mark | 1 | 2 | 3 | 4 | 5 | 6 | 7 | 8 | 9 |

# Healthy Food Substitutes

What we would really have loved is to have substituted many of our everyday household products for healthier alternatives The main reason being is that natural, non-technically enhanced products are LOADED with essential nutrients that fuel your body, mind and soul. Apart form the obvious short and long term benefits of consuming these ingredients, you can literally taste the difference. However not wanting to isolate those that are not able to purchase these products readily, we did not include these within our recipes, opting instead to add this section, which we feel, is vital to you and your families' health. For those of you able to access these products readily the table below will show you what mainstream ingredient can be easily substituted with a healthier (and less technically altered and therefore nutrient drained) alternative. For more information on this we recommend our good friend Cyndi O'Meara's book *Changing Habits Changing Lives:*

| PRODUCT | SUBSTITUTE |
| --- | --- |
| White Sugar | • Brown sugar<br>• Organic raw sugar* |
| Oil | • Cold pressed extra virgin olive oil*<br>• Cold pressed macadamia nut oil*<br>• Cold pressed walnut oil<br>• Rice bran oil<br>• Sunflower oil |
| Spray Oil | • Cold pressed macadamia nut oil * (or if you can't find, use one of the above oils in your own spray bottle) |
| Flour | • Spelt flour<br>• Organic plain flour<br>• Organic self raising flour |
| Margarine | • Butter |
| Eggs | • Free range eggs* |
| Milk | • Organic milk*<br>• Raw milk (pasteurised only milk) |
| Pasta | • Made from fresh ingredients<br>• Organic Pasta* |
| Honey | • Manuka honey*<br>• Organic honey* |
| Jams | • Organic jam*<br>• Homemade jams made from raw ingredients. |
| Soy Sauce | • Tamari soy sauce* |

*Note — all ingredients with an asterisk * can now be bought in your local supermarket. Where possible buy products labeled 'certified organic' as these products have passed all the stringent tests to ensure that they really are organic and therefore are loaded with nutrients and flavour.*

# Contents

# Breakfasts

*"The strength of a civilization should not be measured by its ability to win wars, but by its ability to prevent them."*

Gene Roddenberry

## A Campfire Egg

**MAKES 4**

- *4 free range eggs*
- *2 oranges*

Cut oranges in half and eat the pulp. Crack an egg into the orange skin and place it in the embers until the egg turns white.

## Basic Crepes

**MAKES 30**

- *3 free range eggs*
- *1½ cups (375ml) milk*
- *2¼ cups (400g) plain flour*
- *1 tsp. sunflower or rice bran oil*

Blend all ingredients (except oil) with 1½ cups (375ml) of water. Heat a non-stick frying pan and add the oil swirling around to coat the entire surface. Pour about ¼ cup of mixture into the pan and swirl in a circular motion outwards so the batter is even. Cook for about 2 minutes or until the bottom is light brown and flip over to cook other side, repeat until mixture is gone.

# Breakfast Dish

**SERVES 4**

- 4 slices bread
- 1 carrot, grated
- 1 cup grated cheese
- 6 free range eggs, beaten

Preheat oven to 180°C. Place bread in a square dish and cover with carrot and beaten eggs, season with sea salt and pepper. Sprinkle cheese on top and bake until the eggs are set and the cheese is melted and bubbling.

*Optional: Substitute carrot for whatever vegetable you like.*

# Baked Raspberry French Toast

**SERVES 6**

**A deliciously different way to prepare French toast.**

- ¾ cup raspberry jam
- 12 slices wholemeal bread, remove crusts
- 6 free range eggs
- 1 cup (250ml) milk

Preheat oven to 220°C. Spread jam on 1 side of 6 slices of bread and cover with remaining bread to form 6 sandwiches. Beat eggs and milk until frothy. Pour just enough egg mixture into well greased pan to cover bottom of a baking dish. Arrange sandwiches in pan. Pour remaining egg mixture over top. Bake in oven for about 20 minutes until golden and egg is set.

# Blueberry Pancakes

**Makes 6**

- *1 cup (175g) self raising flour*
- *1 cup (250ml) soya milk*
- *1 free range egg*
- *½ cup fresh blueberries*

Combine first 3 ingredients in a bowl, add blueberries and mix well. Cook in ¼ cup portions in a non-stick frying pan over medium-low heat. Wait for bubbles to appear before flipping.

*Optional: Fabulous served with citrus-infused maple syrup. To make; simply take half a cup of maple syrup and to it add a large piece of orange peel, allow to sit for flavours to infuse.*


# Cafe Style Scrambled Eggs

**SERVES 2**

**Recipe from Kelly Mauger.**

- *4 free range eggs*
- *½ cup (125ml) pouring cream*

In a microwave-safe dish, beat ingredients and season. Cook for 2½ minutes on high or until it starts to rise. Remove and serve on toast.

# Caramel Bananas

**MAKES 4**

**A recipe by the adorable Brett McCosker.**

- *4 bananas*
- *¾ cup (165g) brown sugar*
- *3 tbs. (45g) butter*
- *4 pancakes*

Cook bananas in butter and sugar over low heat in a non-stick frying pan until bananas are soft and caramelised. Place each pancake on a plate and pour over the mixture.


# Caramelised Croissants

**SERVES 4**

- *4 croissants*
- *1 tbs. (15g) butter*
- *2 large bananas*
- *2 tbs. brown sugar*

Preheat grill to 180°C. Halve each croissant and spread with butter. Top equally with sliced banana and then sprinkle with brown sugar. Grill until golden brown and serve warm.

# Creamy Choc-Strawberry Waffles

**SERVES 9**

- *8 warm waffles*
- *¼ cup (80g) Nutella or Hazelnut spread*
- *¾ cup fresh ricotta*
- *8 big, ripe strawberries, washed, hulled and chopped*

Toast waffles. Combine nutella and ricotta. Spread evenly over waffles and top with strawberries.

# Grilled Fruit with Muesli Yoghurt

**SERVES 4**

- *8 ripe nectarines*
- *2–3 tbs. honey*
- *1 tsp. ground cinnamon*
- *400g tubs of Greek style yoghurt with toasted muesli*

Preheat grill on high. Line a baking tray with foil. Place fruit cut side up, drizzle with honey to lightly coat and sprinkle evenly with cinnamon. Grill until honey bubbles and fruit begins to char. Serve warm with dollops of yoghurt and muesli mix.

*Optional: Substitute nectarines for pears, peaches or whatever fruit is in season. Nearly any Greek yoghurt combination works with this.*

# French Toast

**SERVES 4**

**Recipe by the charming Cyndi O'Meara.**

- *4 pieces of stale bread*
- *4 free range eggs*
- *½ cup (125ml) milk*
- *¼ tsp. mixed spice*

Beat eggs, milk and spice together, soak bread in the mixture, once bread is soaked place into hot non-stick pan and cook on both sides until just golden in colour.

*Optional: Serve with fresh fruit and real maple syrup.*

# Lemon Butter

**A sensational spread for breakfast from the beautiful Dymphna Boholt.**

- *115g butter*
- *½ cup (110g) sugar*
- *3 free range eggs*
- *3 lemons*

Melt butter, add sugar and well-beaten eggs and the juice of the lemons. Cook over gentle heat until thick. Pour into jar and store in fridge.

*Optional: Grate in the zest of a lemon. For passionfruit butter, omit zest and use ½ cup passionfruit pulp and ¼ cup lemon juice.*

*Hint: In the microwave: Melt butter and sugar. In a separate bowl, beat eggs with a beater until frothy. Juice the lemons and add them and the eggs to the butter mix. Cook on med/high for 5 minutes stirring every minute.*

# Morning Mushies

**SERVES 2**

**A recipe from Jan Neale.**

- *1 tsp. butter*
- *200g mushrooms, sliced*
- *½ cup (125ml) pouring cream*
- *2 slices thick wholemeal bread*

Heat butter in a non-stick frying pan over a moderate heat. Cook mushrooms, stirring, for 3–5 minutes. Add cream and gently stir until sauce thickens. Season to taste with black pepper. Serve over toast.

*Optional: Sprinkle with freshly chopped chives.*

*Hint: Don't peel mushrooms before cooking as most of the flavour and nutritional value is just below the skin.*

# Muesli Smoothie

**SERVES 1–2**

**A recipe from the lovely Kim Morrison.**

- *1 cup (250ml) milk or soy milk*
- *1 frozen banana*
- *½ cup (55g) toasted muesli*
- *3 tbs. fruit yoghurt*

Place all ingredients in blender and process until smooth.

*Optional: Add ice if you would like it colder.*

# Orange & Prune Crunch Cereal

**SERVES 2**

- *200g tub flavoured yoghurt*
- *1 medium orange, peeled*
- *5 medium prunes, stones removed*
- *½ cup (50g) oats*

Place the yoghurt in a medium bowl. Slice the orange flesh thinly and stir into the yoghurt with the prunes and rolled oats.


# Quick Bircher Muesli

**SERVES 1**

**Recipe by Cyndi O'Meara.**

- *¼ cup (25g) oats*
- *1 banana*
- *½ cup strawberry yoghurt*
- *1 tbs. chopped nuts*

Soak oats in water overnight. In the morning, drain, add chopped banana, nuts and yoghurt and combine, served chilled.

*Optional: Add whatever fruit you like.*

# Quick Muffins

**MAKES 6**

- *1 cup (175g) self raising flour*
- *4 tbs. whole egg mayonnaise*
- *¾ cup (185ml) milk*
- *4 bacon rashers, diced and fried*

Preheat oven to 180°C. Mix all ingredients until just combined. Fill muffin cups ⅔ full. Bake in oven for about 15–20 minutes.

*Optional: Substitute bacon for whatever you like.*


# Spinach Dampers

**MAKES 6**

- *250g pkt frozen spinach, chopped and thawed*
- *2 cups (350g) self raising flour*
- *200ml sour cream*

Preheat oven to 220°C. Line a baking tray with paper. Squeeze excess liquid from spinach. Place flour in a bowl and add sour cream, stir to combine. Add spinach and mix by hand to make a sticky dough. Turn out onto a floured surface and kneed until smooth. Shape into 6 balls and place on tray. Bake for 15 minutes.

*Optional: Grated zucchini (courgette), or a can of corn can be used instead of spinach. Top with grated parmesan cheese prior to baking.*

# Sweet Breakfast Toast

**MAKES 1**

**Recipe by Cyndi O'Meara.**

- 1 slice bread
- 1 tsp. peanut butter
- 1 tsp. honey
- 1 small banana, mashed

Toast the bread, first spread with peanut butter, then honey, then banana.

*Optional: Sprinkle with pine nuts.*

# Tomato Jam

- 3 kg ripe tomatoes
- 2 kg sugar
- 4 lemons

Skin tomatoes by scalding for a few minutes in boiling water, place in a large saucepan with sugar, lemon juice and finely shredded rind. Boil rapidly until jam sets when tested. Bottle.

*Hint: If making jam be sure that your jars are heated to seal well. Rest them in hot water and dry quickly before filling each jar.*

# Dips

*"If we could give every individual the right amount of nourishment and exercise, not too little and not too much, we would have found the safest way to health."*

Hippocrates

---

## Bailey's Dip Delight

**SERVES 8**

**This is a favourite for all gatherings by the gorgeous Jules Boag.**

- *¼ cup (65ml) Baileys liqueur*
- *2 tbs. brown sugar*
- *250g sour cream*

Mix all ingredients together and serve with fresh strawberries or slice a fresh pineapple, cut out the core and pour the dip into the centre of the pineapple. Slice the removed core and use as dipping chips.

## Basil Dip

**MAKES 1 CUP**

**Recipe by Laurent Vancam.**

- *1 bunch of fresh basil*
- *2 tsp. minced garlic*
- *75g parmesan cheese, grated*
- *¼ cup (65ml) extra virgin olive oil*

Blend all ingredients together and serve. Easy and ultra tasty.

---

# Cinnamon Dip

**MAKES 1 CUP**

**A sensational recipe by Shane McCosker.**

- *250g sour cream*
- *2 tsp. ground cinnamon*
- *1 tbs. brown sugar*

Place all ingredients into a bowl and mix well. Chill for at least 2 hours prior to serving to allow flavours time to develop. Serve with a platter of fresh fruit and dried apricots for dipping.

# Corn Chips

**MAKES 32**

- *4 corn tortillas, cut into 8 pieces*
- *½ cup (125ml) olive oil*

Place oil in a large saucepan and heat until hot. Cook corn tortillas in batches for 1–2 minutes or until crisp and golden. Drain on soaking paper and sprinkle with sea salt.

# Curried Chutney Dip

**MAKES APPROX. 1 CUP**

- *125g cream cheese*
- *3 tbs. mixed fruit chutney*
- *¼ tsp. curry powder*
- *Freshly cracked pepper*

Mix all ingredients together, chill before serving with your favourite crackers or vegie sticks.

# Date Dip

MAKES 1 CUP

**Rich and delicious.**

- *250g pkt dates*
- *½ cup (160g) sour cream*

Chop dates finely. Bring dates and ½ cup water to boil and simmer for a few minutes until most of the water is absorbed. Cool date mixture then blend thoroughly with cream. Chill for several hours before serving with a mezze of fresh fruit.

# Easy Creamy Dip

MAKES 1 CUP

**A recipe by the dynamic Deb Wheeler.**

- *½ cup (125ml) creamy mayonnaise*
- *½ cup (160g) sour cream*
- *1 garlic clove, crushed*

Mix all ingredients together and serve chilled with fresh broccoli, cauliflower florets or carrot sticks.

*Hint: Always use equal parts mayonnaise and sour cream when making this tasty dip.*

# Feta Dip

**MAKES 1 CUP**

**This is really, really tasty.**

- *200g feta*
- *½ cup (65ml) olive oil*
- *1 garlic clove, crushed*
- *¼ cup (65ml) milk*

Place feta, oil and garlic into a food processor and blend until combined. Whilst still processing, gently add milk in a slow stream and mix until a smooth paste forms. Chill before serving.

*Optional: Serve with melba toast or fresh vegie sticks.*


# Home Style Corn Chips

**SERVES 4**

**A healthier option for your dips by Maz Lacy.**

- *4 slices pita bread*
- *Extra virgin olive oil spray*
- *3 tbs. lemon pepper or garlic salt*

Preheat oven to 160°C. Cut pita bread into corn chip size pieces and spray with olive oil. Sprinkle with lemon pepper and bake for 6–10 minutes or until crispy.

# Melba Toast

**MAKES 16**

- *4 slices of wholemeal bread*

Preheat oven to 180°C. Remove crusts and cut each piece of bread diagonally into quarters. Place on a baking tray and bake for 6 minutes or until lightly golden and crisp.

*Optional: You can roll bread thinner if preferred.*

# Nutty Blue Cheese Dip

**MAKES 1 CUP**

- *250g cream cheese*
- *¼ cup (60g) whole egg mayonnaise*
- *115g stilton cheese, crumbled*
- *4 tbs. chopped walnuts, toasted*

Beat cream cheese and mayonnaise in a bowl until smooth. Add cheese and walnuts. Chill and serve with a mezze of fresh vegie sticks or crackers.

# Parmesan, Caper & Basil Spread

**MAKES 1¼ CUP**

**A recipe from Janelle McCosker.**

- *200g cream cheese, softened*
- *50g parmesan cheese, finely grated*
- *1½ tbs. capers, rinsed and roughly chopped*
- *1½ tbs. finely chopped fresh basil*

Blend cheeses in a bowl. Add capers and basil, season with pepper. Refrigerate for at least 1 hour before serving. This allows time for the flavours to develop.

# Red Yoghurt Dip

**MAKES 1 CUP**

- *55g marinated red peppers, drained*
- *1 cup (250ml) Greek yoghurt*

Puree peppers with yoghurt. Chill and serve with crusty French bread or a mezze of fresh vegie sticks.

# Tapenade

**MAKES APPROX. 1 CUP**

- ⅔ cup kalamata olives
- 1 clove garlic, crushed
- 2 tbs. finely chopped, fresh basil
- 1½ tbs. olive oil

Place ingredients in a blender and process until smooth. Cover, chill and when needed, serve with crackers.

# Salmon Savoury Log

**SERVES 6–8**

- 415g can pink salmon
- 2 spring onions, finely chopped
- 125g feta cheese
- ½ cup chopped parsley

Drain salmon and remove bones. Crumble feta cheese and combine with salmon, add spring onions. Shape into a log and roll in parsley. Chill and serve with slices of cucumber or melba toast.

*Hint: Parsley is the world's most popular herb. It contains three times as much vitamin C as oranges, twice as much iron as spinach, is rich in vitamin A and contains folate, potassium and calcium.*

# Toblerone Dip

**MAKES 1 CUP**

**A recipe from the lovely Donna McCosker that will have your guests asking for more!**

- *100g Toblerone*
- *2 tbs. pouring cream whipped to soft peaks*
- *1 tbs. honey*

In microwave jug, melt Toblerone on low heat for approx. 2 minutes, stirring every 15 seconds. Cool, then mix through cream and honey and serve with a mezze of fresh fruit to dip.

*Hint: When recipe calls for spoonfuls of honey or golden syrup use a spoon that's been dipped in hot water. The mixture will slip off the spoon more easily.*

# Warm Cheese Dip

**MAKES 2 CUPS**

**This is R.e.a.l.l.y Y.u.m.m.y!!!**

- *2 tbs. (30g) butter*
- *¾ cup (240g) sour cream*
- *250g cheddar cheese, grated*
- *½ tsp. ground cumin*

Melt butter in saucepan and add cumin, stir over a low heat for a minute. Add sour cream and when warm, add cheddar cheese. Stir constantly until the cheese melts and the mixture is smooth. Serve warm with crackers or fresh crusty bread.

# Salad Dressings

*The most important thing in life is to know when to seize opportunities and when to abandon interests.*

Someone wise!

---

## Apricot & Tahini Dressing

**MAKES ¾ CUP**

**Recipe by Gabrielle Bluett.**

- 2 tbs. apricot jam
- ½ cup (120g) tahini
- 1 tsp. mustard
- 1–2 tbs. rice vinegar

Mix all ingredients together.

## Balsamic Dressing

**MAKES 1 CUP**

**Recipe by Tracey Stevens who describes it as "A yummy, creamy dressing."**

- 100ml (slightly less than ½ cup) rice bran oil
- 2 tsp. Dijon mustard
- ⅓ cup (80ml) milk
- 2 tbs. balsamic vinegar

Mix the oil, mustard and milk together in a screw top jar and shake to combine. Add the balsamic vinegar and shake again.

# Blue Cheese Dressing

**MAKES 1 CUP**

- *30g stilton cheese*
- *⅓ cup (80g) whole egg mayonnaise*
- *⅓ cup (80g) natural yoghurt*
- *3 tbs. freshly chopped chives*

Mash stilton in a small bowl using a fork. Add remaining ingredients and mix well. Season to taste with black pepper.


# Buttermilk Dressing

**MAKES ½ CUP**

**Recipe by Gabrielle Bluett.**

- *⅓ cup (80ml) buttermilk*
- *1 tbs. balsamic vinegar*
- *1 tbs. lemon juice*
- *½ tsp. mustard*

Mix all ingredients thoroughly and refrigerate in a tightly sealed jar.

# Classic Salad Dressing

**MAKES 1 CUP**

**Forever stands the test of time!**

- ¼ cup (60ml) fresh lemon juice
- 2 tbs. extra virgin olive oil
- 1 tsp. Dijon mustard
- 1 clove garlic, crushed

Place all in a screw top jar, season to taste and shake well.

*Hint: When a jar of mustard is nearly empty, add some olive oil and wine vinegar and shake well for a delicious salad dressing.*


# Caramelised Balsamic Vinegar

**MAKES APPROX. ½ CUP**

- ⅔ cup (160ml) balsamic vinegar
- ½ cup (110g) brown sugar

Bring ingredients to the boil slowly. Stir until sugar dissolves. Boil until slightly thick. Allow to cool and store in refrigerator.


# Easy Salad Dressing

**MAKES ½ CUP**

- 2 tbs. lemon juice
- ¼ cup (60ml) olive oil

Mix well lemon juice and oil and season with sea salt and pepper.

# Feta Dressing

**MAKES APPROX. 1 CUP**

- *100g feta cheese, crumbled finely*
- *1 clove garlic, crushed*
- *½ cup (125ml) French salad dressing*

Place all ingredients in a jar and shake vigorously.

# Flavoured Oils

**CHILLI**

- *20 seeded and chopped chillies*
- *2 cups (500ml) extra virgin olive oil*

Place chillies into a heatproof container. Heat oil in a small frying pan until it just reaches smoking point, leave to cool for 10 minutes then pour over the chillies and leave for at least 1½ hours. Strain into a clean bottle and keep in refrigerator.

**GARLIC**

- *1 garlic clove, peel and halved*
- *2 cups (500ml) extra virgin olive oil*

Peel and halve a large garlic clove and place in a clean bottle with the olive oil. Seal tightly and store in a cool place for 2 weeks.

**ROSEMARY**

- *2–3 stems of fresh rosemary*
- *2 cups (500ml) extra virgin olive oil*

Submerge rosemary in oil in a bottle. Seal tightly and store in a cool place for 2 weeks.

# Orange & Mustard Dressing

**MAKES 2 CUPS**

- ¾ cup (185ml) orange juice
- ⅓ cup (85ml) Dijon mustard
- 1 cup (250ml) olive oil

Whisk all ingredients together, season with sea salt and pepper.


# Poppy Seed Dressing

**MAKES APPROX. ½ CUP**

**Inspired by Jodie Branche.**

- 1 tbs. poppy seeds
- 4 tbs. organic honey
- 4 tbs. sunflower oil

Put all ingredients in a squirt bottle or jar and shake. Serve over salad. Store in fridge when not in use.


# Queenie's Mayonnaise

**MAKES APPROX. 2 CUPS**

**A recipe from Queenie Bermingham.**

- 400g can condensed milk
- 2 tsp. dry mustard
- ½ – ¾ cup (120 – 180ml) white or brown vinegar

Pour condensed milk into a jar and add mustard stirring well. Add ½ cup of vinegar and mix thoroughly. Add remaining vinegar if needed.

# Raita

**MAKES 2 CUPS**

- *1 cup (250g) plain yoghurt*
- *1 small cucumber, finely chopped*
- *1 tbs. chopped fresh mint*
- *1 small vine-ripened tomato, diced*

Mix all ingredients together and season well.


# Sweet Chilli Dressing

**SERVES 4**

**Recipe by Tracey Stevens.**

- *100ml extra virgin olive oil*
- *1 tbs. whole grain mustard*
- *1 tbs. sweet chilli sauce*
- *⅓ cup (85ml) white vinegar*

Combine all ingredients in a screw top jar and shake to combine.

*Optional: Add a clove of garlic and 1 tsp. brown sugar if you have them.*

# Sauces

*Inspiration follows aspiration.*

Rabindranath Tagore

---

## Aioli

**MAKES APPROX. ½ CUP**

- *½ cup (130g) whole egg mayonnaise*
- *1 garlic clove, crushed*
- *2 tbs. lemon juice*

Mix all together, season with sea salt and pepper and chill for several hours before serving, allowing time for flavours to infuse.

*Optional: Add ½ tsp. mustard and 1 tsp. honey for a difference. Delicious served with almost any seafood dish and hot chips.*

## Chive & Red Pepper Butter

**MAKES APPROX. 1 CUP**

- *¼ cup well drained marinated peppers, chopped*
- *1 tbs. chopped chives*
- *125g butter, softened*

Beat altogether and serve over warm corn on the cob. Great at any bbq.

# Cream Sauce

**MAKES APPROX. 1 CUP**

**Recipe by Gabrielle Bluett.**

- *250ml double cream*
- *2 tsp. Dijon mustard*
- *1 tsp. Horseradish cream (optional)*
- *1 tbs. lemon juice*

Place cream in a saucepan and heat through. Remove from heat before adding all other ingredients and stirring well.

# Green Peppercorn Sauce

**SERVES 2**

- *1½ tsp. green peppercorns*
- *¼ cup (60ml) pouring cream*

Add peppercorns to hot frying pan (if accompanying meat) add to the frying pan after cooking meat. Reduce heat to medium. Cook stirring for 1 minute. Stir in cream. Simmer for 2 minutes or until sauce thickens slightly.

*Hint: This is delicious over steak served with baked potato and vegies.*

# Hollandaise Sauce

**MAKES ¾ CUP**

- *2 free range egg yolks*
- *2 tbs. vinegar*
- *125g butter, melted*

Place egg yolks and 2 tbs. vinegar in a food processor whisking until blended. Add butter slowly until thick and creamy, season with a pinch of sea salt and cracked pepper.

*Optional: Serve warm over an English muffin with crispy bacon or salmon and a poached egg.*


# Hot Fudge Sauce

**MAKES 1 CUP ... You'll wish it made more!**

- *200g dark chocolate, chopped*
- *1 cup white marshmallows, chopped*
- *1 cup (250ml) pouring cream*

Combine all ingredients in a microwave dish and heat on high stirring every 30 seconds until blended.

*Optional: Serve drizzled over the peanut butter ice cream pie (see Desserts).*

# Lemon & Lime Reduction

**MAKES 1 CUP**

**A recipe by Kelly Mauger.**

- *2 cups (400g) caster sugar*
- *2 whole lemons*
- *2 whole limes*
- *A sprinkle of chilli flakes*

Pour 2 cups (500ml) of water into a saucepan along with sugar, lemons and limes and bring to the boil. Reduce to a simmer for about 30 minutes. Remove from heat and take out whole lemons and limes, add chilli flakes to taste and allow to cool.

*Hint: This is fabulous served over just about any fish or seafood dish.*


# Mango Yoghurt Sauce

**MAKES 1 CUP**

- *200g plain yoghurt*
- *3 tbs. mango pulp, canned or fresh*
- *1 tsp. honey*

Combine all ingredients and serve over ice-cream or fruit Salad.

*Optional: For a sensational savoury version, replace honey with chilli powder or tabasco sauce and serve as a sauce or marinade for chicken, fish or meat.*

# Mint Sauce

**Makes a lovely glaze served over roast lamb.**

- *2 tbs. finely chopped mint*
- *2 tbs. lemon juice*
- *1 tbs. sugar*

Place all ingredients plus 4 tbs. boiling water into a small saucepan and cook over a low heat for 5 minutes. Allow to stand for 30 minutes before serving.


# Plum Sauce

**MAKES ½ CUP**

**Recipe by Gabrielle Bluett.**

- *6 tsp. plum jam*
- *2 tsp. grated ginger*
- *2 tsp. sesame oil*
- *2 tbs. rice vinegar*

Mix all ingredients in a saucepan on a very low heat and serve warm.


# Salsa

**MAKES 1 CUP**

- *1 avocado, diced*
- *1 tsp. finely chopped red chilli*
- *Juice of ½ lime*
- *¼ cup diced red pepper*

Combine altogether (may need a little more lime juice) and serve over grilled fish or pork.

# Satay Sauce

**MAKES ½ CUP**

**Recipe by Gabrielle Bluett.**

- *2 tbs. crunchy peanut butter*
- *2 tbs. Tamarind chilli sauce*
- *1 tbs. coconut milk powder*

Mix all ingredients well with ¼ cup of water and heat in a saucepan on a low heat.

# Stilton Butter

**MAKES ½ CUP**

**Recipe by Jan Neale.**

- *200g stilton cheese*
- *125g butter, softened*
- *¼ cup finely chopped parsley*
- *1 tsp. lemon juice*

Process all ingredients in a food processor for 30 seconds or until well mixed. Serve with warm, crusty bread ... Yummy!

# Cocktail Food

*Choose your Attitude!*

Inside of a lift at Radio National, Auckland N.Z.

## Asparagus Wraps

**MAKES APPROX. 16**

**These are absolutely DIVINE.**

- *2 bunches asparagus, ends trimmed*
- *8 slices prosciutto*
- *2 tbs. extra virgin olive oil*

Preheat oven to 180°C. Use a sharp knife to cut the prosciutto lengthways into thin, long strips. Wrap a piece of prosciutto around each asparagus spear, creating a long, spiral effect. Place each spear on baking tray, drizzle with oil and season with sea salt and pepper. Bake for 5–6 minutes.

# Baked Haloumi

**A recipe from Jane Saunders, Whangarei N.Z.**

- *2 tbs. plain flour*
- *250g pkt haloumi cheese, drained and cut into 3cm cubes*
- *3 tbs. extra virgin olive oil*
- *2 tbs. fresh lemon juice*

Place flour on small plate, season with sea salt and pepper and evenly coat haloumi. Heat oil in non-stick frying pan over high heat. Add haloumi and turn occasionally for 2 minutes or until golden brown. Transfer to serving plate, sprinkle with lemon juice and season with pepper.

# Cheddar & Thyme Wafers

**MAKES 10**

**Recipe by Wendy King.**

- *250g cheddar cheese, grated*
- *100g parmesan cheese, shaved*
- *10 sprigs fresh thyme*

Preheat oven to 180°C. Combine cheeses and on a baking paper lined tray, make 10 circles with cheeses, top with fresh thyme leaves. Bake for 12–15 minutes until golden brown. Remove from tray and place on absorbent paper to soak up excess oil. After a couple of minutes coil cheese wafers over rolling pin or narrow glass to make curled shape. Use wafers for dips or garnish for a salad.

# Cheese Triangles

**MAKES 12**

**Always a winner served with sweet chilli sauce to dip.**

- *500g Feta cheese*
- *3 free range eggs, beaten*
- *375g filo pastry*
- *125g butter, melted*

Preheat oven to 200°C. Crumble feta in a bowl and add eggs, season and mix well. Remove 1 sheet of pastry and brush with melted butter. Place second sheet on top and brush with butter, repeat with third sheet. Cut pastry into 4 lengthwise strips (each of these 4 strips will make one triangle). Place 2 tsp. of cheese mixture onto edge of each strip. Fold into a triangle and keep folding maintaining the triangle shape. Place on a paper lined oven tray and bake for 20 minutes.

# Chicken Vol-Au-Vonts

**MAKES 30 SMALL OR 6 LARGE**

- *Vol-au-vont cases*
- *525g bottle Chicken Tonight, honey mustard*
- *125g shredded cheese*
- *2 double chicken breast fillets, diced*

Preheat oven to 180°C. Dice chicken and cook in a non-stick frying pan till lightly browned. Turn down heat and add chicken tonight, stir to heat through. Place vol-au-vont shells on a lined baking tray and fill each with chicken mixture. Top with cheese and place in oven for 15 minutes or until cheese has bubbled and melted. Serve with salad or vegetables of choice.

*Optional: Cut 10 rounds from 2 sheets of ready rolled puff pastry and blind bake instead of using vol-au-vent shells.*

# Chipolata Rolls with Spicy Tomato Sauce

**MAKES 8**

- *2 sheets frozen ready rolled puff pastry*
- *8 chipolata sausages*
- *⅔ cup (190ml) tomato sauce*
- *2 tbs. Worcestershire sauce*

Preheat oven to 220°C. Cut pastry sheets into quarters. Wrap pastry around the centre of each sausage. Brush edges of pastry with water and press to seal. Place sausage rolls, seam down, on a paper lined baking tray. Bake for 18 minutes or until golden brown. Mix sauces together and serve with baked chipolata rolls.


# Creamy Brie

**SERVES 4–6**

- *125g wheel of double brie cheese*
- *1 tbs. raspberry jam*
- *100g flaked almonds, toasted*

Place brie on a microwave safe serving plate, spread with jam and press on almonds to coat. Cook on high for 30 seconds, wait 5 seconds and repeat this process twice to prevent over heating the cheese. Serve with melba toast or your favourite crackers.

*Optional: Use whatever jam you like.*

# Curry Curls

**MAKES 40**

**A tasty delight from Joy Duke.**

- *250g packet potato crisps, finely crushed*
- *2 tsp. curry powder*
- *4 sheets ready rolled puff pastry*

Preheat oven to 200°C. Combine chips and curry powder in a bowl. Sprinkle one pastry sheet with mixture. Place a sheet of pastry on top and press down firmly. Cut into 2cm strips and twist to curl, laying on a baking paper lined tray. Repeat with remaining pastry and mixture. Bake for 15–20 minutes or until golden brown.

*Hint: Working with very cold ready rolled puff pastry prevents the pastry stretching when cut.*


# Fried Calamari

**SERVES 4**

**Y.U.M ... Y.U.M ... Y.U.M!!!**

- *4 fillets of whole fresh squid cleaned and cut into 2 cm rings or strips*
- *½ cup (125ml) sunflower oil*
- *3 cups (525g) plain organic flour*
- *¾ cup (100g) vegetable seasoning*

Pat squid dry with absorbent paper and heat oil in a large non-stick frying pan. Combine flour and seasoning, toss calamari through and shake excess off before frying quickly in very hot oil until tender (about 2 minutes). Lay on paper to absorb excess oil and serve with a sprinkle of sea salt.

*Optional: Divine served with Aioli (see Sauces).*

# Goats Cheese & Sundried Tomato Tarts

**MAKES 8**

- *250g Goats cheese*
- *100g sundried tomatoes*
- *8 individual uncooked pastry cases*
- *4 basil leaves*

Pre-heat oven to 180°C. Fill uncooked pastry cases with chopped sundried tomatoes, chopped basil and crumbled fresh goats cheese. Bake for 15 minutes or until cheese melts.

# Mini Roasted Pepper Tartlets

**MAKES 10**

- *1 sheet ready rolled puff pastry, thawed*
- *250g tub roasted pepper dip*
- *5 slices of char-grilled marinated peppers, chopped coarsely*
- *¼ cup fresh basil leaves*

Preheat oven to 200°C. Using a scone cutter cut 10 rounds into sheet of pastry. Line fairy cake tin holes (may need greasing if not non-stick). Divide dip equally into rounds, top with peppers and bake for 15 minutes. Remove, allow to cool slightly and top with fresh basil leaves. Serve warm.

# Mini Salmon Cream Quiche

**MAKES 24**

- *2 x 115g smoked salmon pate*
- *½ cup (125ml) milk*
- *3 free range eggs*
- *2 sheets ready rolled puff pastry*

Preheat oven to 200°C. Cut 9 rounds with a scone cutter from each sheet of pastry, combine excess and roll to cut a further 6 rounds. Line a non-stick 12 hole fairy cake tin. In a bowl or blender, mix first 3 ingredients. Pour mixture into each and bake for 30 minutes or until filling is puffed and pastry golden. Repeat the process for the next dozen. Allow to stand for 10 minutes before removing from tray.

*Optional: Season with pepper and top with a sprig of fresh dill or the zest of a lemon. Substitute pate for smoked salmon cream cheese.*

# Olive Triangles

**MAKES 16**

- *Extra virgin olive oil spray*
- *100g pitted kalamata olives, chopped*
- *60g semi-dried tomatoes, chopped*
- *1 sheet frozen ready rolled puff pastry*

Preheat oven to 200°C. Lightly grease a baking tray with oil. Combine olives and tomatoes and evenly spread the mixture over the pastry, pressing gently. Cut pastry into quarters and then again diagonally forming four triangles per quarter. Place onto tray and bake for 12 minutes or until crisp and golden.

*Optional: These are delicious served with hummus or your favourite dip.*

# Onions on Horseback

- *1 jar pickled onions*
- *3 slices of bacon, quartered*

Roll each pickled onion in a piece of bacon and fix securely with a damp toothpick. At serving time, grill until bacon is crisp or bake in a hot oven.

*Options:*

- *Devils on Horseback; replace the onion with a pitted prune*
- *Angels on Horseback; replace the onion with an oyster, season with pepper and lemon juice.*


# Parmesan Crisps

**MAKES 6**

**A recipe by Lorraine Leeson.**

- *200g wedge parmesan cheese*
- *1 tbs. sesame seeds*

Preheat oven to 200°C. Line a tray with baking paper and place 6 egg rings on top. Into each, grate enough parmesan to cover the base. Top with a sprinkle of sesame seeds, gently remove egg rings and bake for 8 minutes or until the cheese melts into lacey discs. Allow to cool and serve with your favourite soup or as a nibble with drinks.

*Optional: Substitute sesame seeds with a sprinkle of smokey paprika or a smattering of your favourite fresh herb.*

# Parmesan Shapes

**MAKES 32**

**A recipe by Wendy King.**

- *2 sheets ready rolled puff pastry, thawed*
- *45g parmesan cheese, grated*
- *Sprinkle of garlic salt*

Preheat oven to 180°C. Using a small cookie cutter, cut approx.
16 shapes from each pastry sheet and place them on a baking paper
lined tray. Sprinkle pastry with cheese and garlic salt then bake for
10–15 minutes or until puffed and golden. Serve warm.

# Pear & Melon Prosciutto Wraps

**SERVES 6**

- *1 pear sliced*
- *1 rockmelon sliced*
- *1 pkt sliced prosciutto*
- *Wedges of lemon for garnish*

Wrap slices of fresh pear or rockmelon in wafer thin slices of prosciutto.
Serve on a plate garnished with lemon slices. Fresh and delicious!!!

# Pesto Palmiers

**MAKES 24**

- *2 sheets ready rolled puff pastry, chilled*
- *½ cup (130g) basil pesto*
- *25g parmesan cheese, grated*

Spread each pastry sheet with basil and parmesan and season. Roll up one side until you reach the middle then repeat with the other side. Place both rolls on a paper lined baking tray and freeze for 30 minutes. Remove and slice each into 1cm slices. Bake in a preheated 200°C oven for 15–20 minutes, or until golden brown.

# Ricotta & Prosciutto Baked Pies

**MAKES 12**

**A recipe from the vibrant Perditta O'Connor.**

- *5 slices prosciutto*
- *400g fresh ricotta*
- *6 sprigs fresh thyme, leaves picked*
- *1 bunch chives, chopped*

Preheat oven to 180°C. Line the base and interior of each mini-muffin pan with the prosciutto. Combine ricotta, thyme and chives in a bowl. Distribute mixture evenly into muffin sections and bake for 15 minutes or until set. Remove tray and set aside for another 15 minutes to cool before serving.

*Optional: Season with sea salt and pepper and bake topped with some halved cherry tomatoes.*

# Spicy Cheddar Shortbread

**MAKES APPROX. 40**

**This one is great with drinks before dinner.**

- *2¼ cups (390g) plain flour*
- *250g butter, slightly softened (reserve just a little for greasing)*
- *150g cheddar cheese, grated*
- *¼ tsp. cayenne pepper*

Place all ingredients (except a ¼ cup plain flour) in a food processor or blender. Process using pulse until just combined. Turn out onto a floured surface (use remaining ¼ cup) and shape into a ball. Cut in half and roll each half into a 30cm log about 3 cm in diameter. Wrap in cling film. Chill until firm (35 minutes). Preheat oven to 200°C. Lightly grease a baking tray cut logs into 5 mm thick rounds, place 2–3 cm apart and bake for 15–20 minutes or until golden. Cool completely. Store in an airtight container.

*Optional: Sprinkle with sesame seeds prior to baking.*


# Tempting Mini-Pizzas

**MAKES 12**

- *1 sheet ready rolled puff pastry*
- *2 tbs. pizza sauce*
- *250g tub antipasto mix*
- *100g feta*

Preheat oven to 180°C. Using a scone cutter, cut 12 rounds from the ready rolled puff pastry. Place on a baking paper lined baking tray and brush with pizza sauce. Distribute evenly the antipasto mix and top with a slice of feta. Bake for 15 minutes and serve warm.

*Optional: Substitute pizza sauce with basil pesto, or mix both for an interesting change. Top with whatever you like.*

# Morning & Afternoon Teas

*Time is not measured by the years that you live but by the deeds that you do, and the joy that you give!*

Anonymous

---

## 1,1,1,1, Cake

**A recipe from the poetic Belinda Gillam ... Defines fast & fabulous!**

- *1 cup (120g) dessicated coconut*
- *1 cup (250ml) milk*
- *1 cup (200g) caster sugar*
- *1 cup (175g) self raising flour*

Preheat oven to 180°C. Place all ingredients in a bowl and mix. Line a loaf tin with baking paper and pour mixture in. Bake for 40 minutes.

*Optional: Serve warm with butter or cold with cream cheese icing ... Deliciously simple!*

# 1,2,3,4 Cake

**A recipe from the lovely Tanya Ormsby.**

- *1 cup (230g) butter*
- *2 cups (400g) caster sugar*
- *3 cups (525g) self raising flour*
- *4 free range eggs*

Preheat oven to 140°C. Grease a 22cm cake tin. Using an electric mixer, cream butter and sugar for 5–10 minutes or until pale and fluffy. Add eggs one at a time, beating well between each addition. Fold through sifted flour. Spoon into prepared pan and bake for 1¼ hours (cover with foil if cake is browning too quickly). Cool in tin before turning out.

*Optional: Delicious topped with a layer of freshly whipped cream and fresh strawberries.*


# Amoretti Biscuits

**MAKES 24**

**Recipe from Kate Schenk.**

- *2 cups (340g) almond meal*
- *1 tsp. almond essence*
- *¾ cup (165g) caster sugar*
- *4 free range egg whites*

Preheat oven to 130°C. Combine meal and essence and about ¾ of the caster sugar. Beat the egg whites until stiff, adding the remaining caster sugar gradually. In three lots, fold almond meal into the beaten egg whites. Spoon into a piping bag with a large nozzle, (or plastic zip lock bag with ½ cm hole cut from one corner) and pipe walnut-sized pieces onto lined baking trays. Bake for 40 minutes.

# Apple Slice

**This will impress!**

- 340g pkt vanilla cake mix
- ¾ cup (180g) butter, melted
- 400g can apple
- 200g sour cream

Preheat oven to 180°C. Mix butter and cake mix to a dough.
Spread evenly in a baking paper lined baking dish and bake for
15 minutes. Combine apple and sour cream. Spread evenly over base
and return to oven for another 15 minutes. Remove and sit before
cooling completely in the fridge (this allows the base time to set).
Serve cold.

*Optional: You can sprinkle with cinnamon before the final bake or use
a tin of pie apple with cinnamon instead.*


# Biscuit Pastry

- 1 tbs. sugar
- 1 tbs. soft butter
- 1 free range egg, well beaten
- 1 cup (175g) self raising flour

Beat sugar and butter together, then add egg and mix. Add flour and
roll out for tarts.

# Caramel & Coconut Pies

**SERVES 6–8**

- ¼ cup butter, softened
- 2 cups (240g) desiccated coconut
- 400g tin Carnation caramel
- 1 banana

Preheat oven to 300°C. Mix butter and coconut. Press evenly into 9 inch pie pan. Bake for 30–35 minutes, or until light brown. Allow to cool before filling with caramel and topping with fresh slices of banana.

# Cashew Cream

**A recipe from Kim Morrison who says "This makes a delicious change from cream on cakes, pancakes and desserts!"**

- 1 cup cashew nuts, unsalted
- 3 oranges, peeled and chopped
- 1 apple, cored and peeled
- 1 tbs. honey

Place all ingredients in blender. Process until smooth and creamy. Serve cold.

# Christmas Balls

**MAKES 40**

**A recipe from Margaret Tindale ... Everyone *loooves* these.**

- *4 cups (480g) desiccated coconut*
- *400g can condensed milk*
- *Zest of 1 lemon*
- *100g pkt red glace cherries, finely chopped*

Preheat oven to 180°C. Place coconut, condensed milk and zest in a bowl and mix well. Add cherries and stir until the pink of the cherries runs through the mixture. Using a tsp. roll mixture into balls and place on two paper lined baking trays approx. 3cm apart. Bake in oven for 12–15 minutes, swapping trays half way through, or until balls are lightly browned. Remove and cool before serving.


# Cream Cheese Scones

**MAKES 6**

- *250g cream cheese*
- *125g butter, softened*
- *1 cup (175g) self raising flour*

Preheat oven to 200°C. Mix cream cheese and butter with a beater until combined. Gradually add the flour beating slowly until blended. Roll out on to a floured surface, cut with a scone cutter, arrange so that each is touching the other on a paper lined baking tray and bake for 12–15 minutes or until golden brown.

*Optional: For savoury, add some parmesan cheese or sun-dried tomatoes. For sweet, bake as is top with fresh cream and jam or butter and golden syrup.*

# Custard Creams

**MAKES 32 OR 16 DOUBLED**

**A favourite of the Beattie Family!**

- 250g softened butter
- ½ cup (60g) icing sugar
- 1 cup (175g) plain flour
- ½ cup (60g) custard powder

Preheat oven to 150°C. Beat butter and icing sugar to a cream. Sift flour and custard powder together and gradually add to butter and sugar. Although crumbly, the mixture will roll into balls. Place on paper lined baking tray. Press lightly on each biscuit with a floured fork. Bake for 10 minutes or until pale golden colour.

*Optional: Join together with lemon or passionfruit icing (see Morning and Afternoon Teas).*


# Date Loaf

**A recipe from Mrs. Frasier, Raceview QLD. Absolutely heavenly!**

- 2 tsp. instant coffee
- 375g pkt dates, chopped
- 1 cup (175g) self raising flour
- ¼ cup (65g) flaked almonds

Add coffee to 1 cup (250ml) of boiling water and mix. Pour over dates and soak overnight. Stir in flour. Pour mixture into a paper lined loaf tin, sprinkle with flaked almonds and bake in a preheated 160°C oven for 45 minutes.

*Optional: Serve warm with lashings of butter.*

# Date Scones

**MAKES 12**

**A recipe from Jennette McCosker.**

- *1 cup (250g) chopped dates*
- *300ml pouring cream*
- *4 cups (700g) self raising flour (plus extra for rolling)*
- *1 cup (250ml) ginger ale*

Preheat oven to 200°C. Sift flour into a bowl, create a well before adding remaining ingredients. Stir with a knife until combined. Place on a floured surface and pat into a round shape about an inch thick. Cut with a scone cutter, arrange closely on a paper lined baking tray, and bake for 12–15 minutes or until golden in colour. These can be frozen or for a smaller quantity simply halve the ingredients.

*Hint: When making scones you can add 2 tbs. cornflour and a generous squeeze of lemon juice. The cornflour will make the scones lighter and the lemon juice will help keep them fresher for longer.*

# Easy Fruit Slice

**The same recipe submitted by both Maureen Wall and John Sealy ... It's a goodie!**

- *400g can condensed milk*
- *375g mixed dried fruit*
- *1 cup (175g) self raising flour*

Preheat oven to 160°C. Mix all ingredients together and pour into a baking paper lined baking tray. Bake for 40–45 minutes or until cooked when tested. Allow to cool and slice. Can be kept in freezer for up to one month.

*Optional: For a flavour variation add one cup of coconut to the mixture before baking. This is lovely served topped with lemon icing.*

# Fruit Bran Loaf

- *1 cup (250g) All-bran*
- *1 cup (170g) dried mixed fruit*
- *1½ cup (375ml) milk*
- *1 cup (175g) self raising flour*

Preheat oven to 180°C. Combine bran, mixed fruit and milk in a bowl, stand for 15 minutes. Add flour and mix well until combined. Spoon mixture into a paper lined loaf tin and bake for 40 minutes or until cooked through. Allow to cool in tin then turn out onto wire rack for further cooling. Serve sliced.

# Fruity Cheese Tarts

**MAKES 24**

- *1½ sheets ready rolled shortcrust pastry, cut into small squares*
- *250g cream cheese, softened*
- *¼ cup (50g) caster sugar*
- *1½ cups (255g) dried mixed fruit*

Preheat oven to 180°C. Line non-stick mini muffin tray with pastry squares, bake for 8 minutes or until crusts begin to brown. Combine cheese and sugar, stir in mixed fruit, spoon into cooled shells. Refrigerate for at least ½ hour before serving.

*Optional: Decorate with a slice of fresh fruit or a glace cherry at Christmas time.*

# Honey Icing

- 125g butter, softened
- 1¼ cup (165g) icing sugar
- 1 tbs. milk
- ¼ cup (80g) honey

Beat all ingredients together until light and fluffy.


# Lemon Icing

**A recipe from the beautiful Wendy Beattie.**

- 2 tbs. (30g) soft butter
- ½ cup (60g) icing sugar (may need a little extra)
- 1 tsp. lemon juice

Combine altogether ... How easy is that!

*Hint: If your icing sugar becomes lumpy, remove lumps with rolling pin while still in packet, sift, then store in a tightly sealed container in the refrigerator.*


# Mock Cream # 1

**A recipe from the beautiful Jennette McCosker.**

- 1 cup (120g) icing sugar
- 2 tbs. (30g) soft butter
- 1 tbs. milk
- ¼ tsp. vanilla essence

Combine all ingredients and beat until light and fluffy.

# Mock Cream # 2

- ½ cup (100g) caster sugar
- 125g butter, softened
- 1 tsp. vanilla essence

Combine a third of a cup of water and sugar in a saucepan, stir consistently over heat until sugar is dissolved, increase heat to bring to boil, remove from heat and allow to become completely cold. Beat butter and vanilla until white and fluffy gradually pouring in cold syrup beating constantly.

# Mouth Watering Mini-Cheesecakes

**MAKES 55**

**These are fantastic, a new Bermingham favourite! And you can freeze some for later (if there's any left!!!)**

- 1 pkt Oreos or chocolate/cream biscuits
- 250g cream cheese, softened
- 400g can condensed milk
- 3 tsp. gelatine

Blend oreo biscuits until completely crushed, pour into a bowl and add 2 tbs. of condensed milk and mix. Place fairy cake cases into mini muffin trays. Spoon 1 tbs. of the mixture into each case. Blend cream cheese and condensed milk until smooth. Mix gelatine with 3 tbs. of boiling water and add to cream cheese mix, stir thoroughly. Spoon mixture into the fairy cake cases to cover the biscuit bases and refrigerate till set (at least 2 hours).

*Optional: Serve as is or topped with a sliver of strawberry, kiwi fruit, peach or dollop of raspberry sauce.*

# Passionfruit Icing

- 1 cup (120g) icing sugar
- 1 passionfruit pulp
- 1 tsp. soft butter

Mix all ingredients well, and spread over cake or cupcakes.


# Peanut Crisps

**MAKES 16**

**A recipe from the beautiful Lorraine Leeson.**

- 1 cup (250ml) condensed milk
- ½ cup (130g) peanut butter
- 3 cups (360g) cornflakes

Preheat oven to 180°C. Combine condensed milk and peanut butter before adding cornflakes. Place spoonfuls on a paper lined baking tray and bake for 15–20 minutes.


**A variation from Joy Duke, makes 40:**

- 400g can condensed milk
- ½ cup (130g) peanut butter
- 3 cups (360g) desiccated coconut
- 1 cup (150g) unsalted nuts, chopped

Preheat oven to 180°C. Mix condensed milk and peanut butter thoroughly. Stir in coconut and nuts. Drop heaped tsp. onto paper lined baking trays. Bake for 15 minutes or until golden brown.

# Pear Cake

**A recipe from the adorable Brett McCosker ... Very easy and very nice!**

- *400g can pears*
- *340g pkt vanilla cake mix*
- *2 free range eggs*

Preheat oven to 180°C. Place pears and liquid into a mixing bowl, add cake mix and eggs. Beat on low speed for 30 seconds, then on high for 4 minutes. Pour mixture into a paper lined 22cm cake tin and bake for 55 minutes or until inserted skewer comes out clean.

*Optional: Delectable served with mock cream and sprinkled with coconut.*


# Pikelets

**MAKES 10**

- *1 free range egg*
- *4 tsp. sugar*
- *1 cup (175g) self raising flour*
- *½ cup (125ml) milk*

Beat egg and sugar together before adding the other ingredients, mix thoroughly. Heat a non-stick frypan and dollop a heaped tbs. of the mixture into it. Flip pikelet when you see small bubbles forming on its upper side. Cook for a further minute and repeat until the mixture is used.

*Optional: Serve with butter, cream, jam, fruit or syrup.*

# Pineapple Tart

**Recipe by Joy Duke, a birthday favourite of her children.**

- *1 sheet ready rolled shortcrust pastry*
- *400g can crushed pineapple*
- *¼ cup (30g) custard powder*
- *1½ cups (375ml) milk*

Preheat oven to 180°C. Place pastry in a tart dish and bake for 10–12 minutes or until lightly golden, remove and cool. Gently boil crushed pineapple in saucepan. Combine custard powder and milk and add to crushed pineapple. Stir until thick (10–15 minutes) and pour into pastry shell, allow to cool and set for 2 hours.

*Optional: Decorate with fresh whipped cream and grated chocolate or fresh fruit.*


# Raisin Loaf

**A recipe from the quirky Kt Anbeck ... *Yummy!***

- *1 tbs. butter (a little extra for greasing)*
- *1 cup (200g) caster sugar*
- *1 cup (170g) raisins*
- *2 cups (350g) self raising flour*

Preheat oven to 180°C. Place butter, sugar and raisins in a saucepan with 1 cup water and bring to boil. Reduce heat and simmer for 5 minutes, set aside and allow to cool. Add flour and mix well. Bake in a greased loaf tin for 45 minutes.

*Optional: Cut into thick slices and serve with butter.*

# Savoury Scones

**MAKES 12**

**This clever recipe was learnt at a 612 ABC Brisbane Breakfast Radio interview - Thanks Majella!**

- *4 cups (700g) self raising flour*
- *300ml double cream*
- *1 cup (250ml) soda water*
- *½ cup semi-dried tomatoes, chopped*

Preheat oven to 200°C. Sift self raising flour into a bowl, make a well and pour in cream and soda water then add tomatoes and season. Mix to make a firm dough, roll out on a floured surface and pat into a round shape about an inch thick. Cut with a scone cutter, place on a paper lined baking tray so that the scones are touching and bake for about 12 minutes or until golden brown.

*Optional: Sprinkle with parmesan cheese before baking. Substitute tomatoes with capers, bacon, olives, corn or fresh herbs.*

# Spicy Fruit Mince Tarts

**MAKES 6**

**You'll be surprised and delighted!**

- *6 slices raisin bread, crusts removed*
- *2 tbs. butter*
- *A jar of your favourite fruit mince*

Butter bread on both sides and cut rounds large enough to line a muffin tray. Cook in a 180°C oven for 3–5 minutes, remove and fill with fruit mince, return to oven for 5 minutes or until edges of bread are a light golden brown.

*Optional: Dust with icing sugar or a dollop of whipped cream for serving.*


# Sponge Cake

**A second generation recipe from Jill McIver.**

- *4 free range eggs (room temperature)*
- *¾ cup (150g) caster sugar*
- *Dash vanilla essence*
- *¾ cup (130g) self raising flour, sifted 5 times*

Preheat oven to 210°C. Beat eggs and sugar with and electric beater for 15 minutes. Add vanilla just before beating completes. Gently fold in flour with a spatula until combined. Line a rectangular baking tin with baking paper, pour mixture in, place in oven and bake for approx. 14 minutes. Remove, cool, cut in half and serve with jam and freshly whipped cream either as a single layer or double.

*Hint: During the cooking of a cake, if the top starts to over-brown, cover loosely with foil.*

# Vanilla Slice

**A s.c.r.u.m.p.t.i.o.u.s recipe from the delightful Val Savage.**

- *1 pkt cream crackers*
- *600ml double cream*
- *50g pkt vanilla pudding mix*

Place a layer of crackers on the bottom of a paper lined rectangular baking dish. Mix cream and pudding together until thick, pour onto biscuit base and top with another layer of biscuits. Refrigerate for at least 30 minutes before slicing and serving.

*Optional: When in season, add two fresh mangoes peeled and sliced to the mixture. This is delicious topped with Passionfruit Icing.*


# Versatile Fruit Cake

**A recipe by the lovely Mai Spoor.**

- *400ml can coconut milk*
- *375g pkt mixed dried fruit*
- *1 cup (175g) self raising flour*

Soak fruit in coconut milk overnight. Add self raising flour and mix well. Bake in a paper lined loaf tin on 125°C for approx. 2 hours or until cooked through.

**A recipe by the effervescent Royelle McDonald.**

- *2 cups (500ml) chocolate flavoured milk*
- *1 kg pkt mixed dried fruit*
- *2 cups (350g) self raising flour*

Soak fruit in milk overnight. Add self raising flour and mix well. Bake in a paper lined 22cm cake tin on 125°C for approx. 2–2½ hours or until cooked through.

**A recipe by Joy Duke.**

- *800g can mangoes*
- *1 kg pkt mixed dried fruit*
- *2 cups (350g) self raising flour*

Soak fruit in mango juice and chopped flesh overnight. Add self raising flour and mix well (may need a little more liquid). Bake in a paper lined 22cm cake tin on 125°C for approx. 2–2½ hours or until cooked through.

**Glen Turnbull's favourite Fruit Cake, recipe from Sr. Jeanette Collis.**

- *2 tbs. instant coffee*
- *1 kg pkt mixed dried fruit*
- *150g block fruit and nut chocolate, roughly chopped*
- *2 cups (350g) self raising flour*

Make 2 cups coffee with instant coffee and boiling water, add to fruit and soak overnight. Add chocolate and flour and mix well. Bake in a paper lined 22cm cake tin on 125°C for approx. 2–2½ hours or until cooked through.

*Hint: All these fruit cakes can be frozen.*

# Light Meals & Lunches

*The trouble with a diet is often you don't eat what you like,
and don't like what you eat.*

An unsuccessful dieter!!!!

# Soups

## Bacon & Pea Soup

**SERVES 4**

**This is really tasty!**

- *1 kg bacon bones*
- *200g pkt dried peas*
- *2 onions, roughly chopped*

Place all ingredients in a large saucepan with 10 cups water. Bring to boil and then simmer for 1 hour. Remove from heat and allow to cool. Remove bacon from bones. If soup is too thick add more water. Blend and serve with a crusty loaf of bread.

# Cauliflower Soup

**SERVES 4**

**A recipe from Jennette McCosker.**

- *A small fresh cauliflower*
- *300ml pouring cream*
- *1 tbs. oyster sauce*

Place chopped cauliflower in a saucepan with 2 cups water and cook until tender. Allow to cool before blending. Mix in cream and oyster sauce and season well. Serve warm.

# Chorizo & Red Pepper Soup

**THIS SERVES 6 and is realllllly tasty!**

- *2 chorizo sausages, diced*
- *4 red peppers, diced*
- *400g can whole peeled tomatoes*
- *3 cups (750ml) chicken stock*

Fry chorizo in a non-stick pan for 5 minutes, remove from pan and set aside. Into the same pan with chorizo juices add peppers and fry for 5 minutes before adding tomatoes. Mix well, season with sea salt and pepper, add stock and bring to boil. Reduce heat and simmer until peppers are tender. Puree the soup and serve sprinkled with chorizo pieces.

# Curry Pumpkin Soup

**SERVES 4**

- 1 kg pumpkin, peeled and chopped
- 1 generous tsp. curry powder
- 1 clove garlic, crushed
- 150ml double cream

Place pumpkin, curry and garlic in a saucepan and add 2 cups of water. Season with sea salt and pepper if you like, bring to boil then reduce heat and simmer for 20 minutes or until pumpkin is tender. Blend before adding cream, stir through and serve.

*Hint: Give plain pumpkin soup a lift by stirring in a ¼ cup crunchy peanut butter and a handful of chopped coriander to each litre of soup.*

# Pumpkin, Lentil & Ginger Soup

**SERVES 4**

- ½ cup red lentils, rinsed
- 1 kg butternut pumpkin, cut into chunks
- 1 tbs. grated ginger
- 1 ltr. vegetable stock

Place all ingredients into a large saucepan, season with sea salt and pepper if you like and cook on a medium heat for 30 minutes. Blend and serve.

# Smoked Salmon & Corn Chowder

**SERVES 6**

**A recipe from the lovely Katrina Price.**

- *1.25 ltr fish stock*
- *400g sweet potato, peeled and chopped*
- *225g can creamed corn*
- *350g can smoked salmon*

Place stock and potato in a saucepan and bring to boil, reduce heat and simmer until potato is cooked. Add corn and salmon and continue to simmer for 5 minutes then blend until smooth. Serve warm.

# Sweet Potato Soup

**SERVES 4**

**A recipe from Rebecca Butler.**

- *2 cups (500ml) chicken stock*
- *½ cup finely chopped onion*
- *2 cups mashed sweet potato*
- *¼ cup (80g) sour cream*

Over a low heat, cook onion in a non-stick pan until golden. Add stock and mash and bring to the boil, stirring until nice and smooth. Reduce heat and simmer for 10 minutes, add sour cream with a few minutes remaining.

*Optional: Garnish with fresh coriander and season to taste. Chicken stock can be replaced with vegetable stock.*

# Tomato Soup

**SERVES 4**

**Recipe from Michelle Dodd "Light & Licious!"**

- *16 Roma tomatoes*
- *2 tbs. extra virgin olive oil*
- *4 sprigs fresh thyme*
- *1 ltr. vegetable stock*

Preheat oven to 180°C. Slice tomatoes in half, place on a foil lined baking tray cut side up and drizzle with oil. Season with sea salt, pepper and thyme. Bake in oven for 40 minutes. Remove and allow to cool slightly. Blend tomatoes and vegie stock. Pour into a saucepan and simmer for 15 minutes. Serve warm with fresh, crusty bread.

# Vegetable Croutons

**SERVES 4**

**A recipe by Lorraine Leeson.**

- *¼ cup (60ml) extra virgin olive oil*
- *1 small sweet potato or parsnip, peeled and diced*
- *1 clove garlic, crushed*

Heat oil in a large pan. Add the vegetables and cook for 10 minutes or until tender and lightly browned. Add garlic in remaining minutes so as not to burn. Drain on paper and sprinkle over soup.

*Hint: If any of your hot soups end up slightly salty, add to it a whole, peeled potato and simmer for about 15 minutes to absorb salt. Remove the potato and serve.*

# All Others

*Everything has its beauty, but not everyone sees it.*

Confucius

---

## Banana & Bacon Melt

**SERVES 2**

**A recipe by Marg Morters, Central Coast NSW.**

- *2 bacon rashers, chopped*
- *4 slices wholemeal bread*
- *1 large banana*
- *65g cheddar cheese, grated*

Fry bacon until crisp. Toast bread under grill on one side only. Slice banana length ways and place on untoasted side of bread and sprinkle with bacon. Top with grated cheese and place under hot grill until cheese has melted and is bubbly.

*Optional: Cut into fingers before serving.*

*Topping Options:*
- *Bacon, pineapple and cheese*
- *Ham, corn, pineapple and cheese*
- *Chicken, asparagus and cheese*
- *Chicken, semi-dried tomatoes and feta*
- *Chicken, avocado and cheese*
- *Ham, asparagus, pineapple and cheese*
- *Salami, antipasto and cheese*

# Bbq Chicken Burgers

**MAKES 4**

- ½ cooked bbq chicken, chopped
- 1 cup (130g) wholegrain breadcrumbs
- ½ cup (160g) sour cream (may need a little more)
- 4 hamburger buns

Preheat oven to 180°C. Mix chicken, breadcrumbs and sour cream together and season with sea salt and pepper. Roll into burgers and bake for 20 minutes. Serve in buns with lots of salad and bbq sauce.

*Optional: Place on a hot bbq with a little olive oil and cook for 4 minutes or until golden brown then flip and cook for a further 3 minutes.*

# Bbq Chicken Pizza

**MAKES 1**

**Recipe from Rodger Fishwick.**

- 1 pita pocket
- 1–2 tbs. bbq sauce
- ½ cooked bbq chicken, chopped
- ¼ cup grated mozzarella cheese

Preheat oven to 180°C. Take a pita pocket and spread bbq sauce evenly over the top. Add chicken and sprinkle with mozzarella cheese. Place on foil lined baking tray and bake for 10 minutes.

# Chicken Nachos

**SERVES 6**

**A sensational footy nibble that everyone can enjoy ... Just ask Paul Bermingham.**

- *1 large pkt plain corn chips*
- *300g cheddar cheese, grated*
- *2 cups (500g) cooked chicken, pulled apart into small pieces*
- *2 tbs. bbq sauce or sweet chilli sauce*

Preheat oven to 160°C. Spread a layer of corn chips on an oven-proof plate. Sprinkle with chicken and cheese followed by a squirt of sauce. Continue process until chicken is all gone and end with ½ cup of cheese. Bake in oven for 10 minutes to melt cheese, then serve. Can also melt in microwave.

*Optional: Top with Guacamole – Yum!!!*


# Cheese Panini

**SERVES 1–2**

- *2 slices panini bread*
- *1 tomato, sliced*
- *1 sprig thyme*
- *2 slices Swiss cheese*

Grill panini on one side and remove when lightly toasted. Flip and top with sliced tomato and fresh thyme. Season before adding cheese. Grill until cheese has melted.

# Curried Tuna Rollups

**SERVES 4**

- *14 slices wholemeal bread, crusts removed*
- *1 cup grated cheese*
- *1 tsp. curry powder*
- *200g can tuna chunks*

Preheat oven to 180°C. Roll bread with a rolling pin to flatten. Combine remaining ingredients and spread on bread, roll and secure with toothpicks. Place rolls on a baking tray and bake for 15 minutes. Cut each roll in half and serve hot.

*Optional: ½ cup softened butter can be used instead of cheese. Brush rolls with melted butter before cooking for a golden brown finish.*

# Curry Pies

**SERVES 4**

**Fast and Fabulous!**

- *8 slices of wholegrain bread, crusts removed*
- *¼ cup (60ml) milk*
- *400g can sweet curry (or your favourite curry)*

Preheat oven to 180°C. Roll bread with a rolling pin to flatten. Use a teacup to cut a round shape from each slice and press into non-stick fairy cake tin. Brush with milk and bake in oven until crisp and golden. Heat sweet curry and spoon into cases. Serve immediately

*Optional: Add in small pieces of leftover chicken, roast meat or vegies.*

*Hint: Grate excess bread to use as bread crumbs and freeze until required.*

# Ham & Cheese Muffins

**MAKES 12**

**A recipe from Lisa Logan.**

- *2 cups (350g) self raising flour*
- *1½ cups (375ml) milk*
- *1 cup grated cheddar cheese*
- *125g ham, chopped*

Preheat oven to 180°C. Sift flour and make a well in the middle, pour in milk, cheese and two thirds of the chopped ham. Mix until combined. Spoon into 12 large muffin tins and place a little of the remaining chopped ham on top of each one. Bake for 25 minutes or until tops are golden brown.

*Optional: These can be frozen.*


# Hot Salmon Puffs

**MAKES 8**

- *200g can red salmon, drained*
- *4 salad onion tops, finely chopped*
- *⅓ cup (80ml) pouring cream*
- *2 sheets ready rolled puff pastry, thawed*

Preheat oven to 180°C. Place salmon, salad onion tops and cream in a saucepan stirring over low heat until thickened. Season with pepper and stand until cool. Cut each sheet of pastry into quarters and evenly distribute the mixture to a corner. Fold into triangles firmly sealing the edges with a fork. Sprinkle each with water. Place the triangles on a paper lined baking tray and bake for 15–20 minutes or until nicely browned.

# Mexican Style Stuffed Jacket Potatoes

**MAKES 4**

- 4 potatoes, scrubbed
- ½ cup (85g) taco sauce
- ½ cup (160g) sour cream
- 1 avocado, mashed

Preheat oven to 180°C. Pierce each potato several times, wrap in foil and bake in oven for 1 hour or until soft through. Remove, and allow to cool before making a large crisscross slit in each. Divide sauce, cream and avocado among the potatoes and serve.


# Picnic Loaf

**A recipe from Michelle Dodd ... Yummo!**

- 1 Ciabatta loaf (Italian style bread with a hard crust)
- 1 jar antipasto mix, drained
- 1 small tub boccocini cheese, sliced
- Your choice of ham, salami, roasted sweet potato

Cut the ciabatta loaf in half lengthways. Scoop out the bread. Fill one side with the antipasto. Fill the other side with bocconcini, follow with your choice of ham, salami or roasted sweet potato. Place the halves back together, wrap in baking paper and secure the paper with sticky tape. Pop in the fridge with a weight on top eg.,a casserole dish, and leave for 2–3 hours, or overnight if possible. To serve, unwrap and cut into slices.

# Prawn Cocktail

**SERVES 4**

- *16 prawns peeled, de-veined and cooked*
- *2 tbs. mayonnaise*
- *2 tbs. tomato paste*
- *Juice of 1 lemon*

Place prawns in a margarita or large wine glass (a bread plate will also suffice). Mix mayonnaise, tomato paste and lemon juice together, trickle over prawns and serve chilled.

*Optional: Serve with crispy fresh lettuce.*


# Salmon Pizza

**MAKES 5**

- *5 small round pita breads*
- *5 tbs. basil pesto*
- *400g can red salmon, drained and flaked*
- *10 bocconcini rounds, halved*

Preheat oven to 200°C. Spread pita with 1 tbs. of pesto, top with salmon and bocconcini. Bake for 10 minutes.

*Optional: Scatter each pizza with rocket to serve.*

# Satay Beef Pizza

**MAKES 1**

**Recipe from Rodger Fishwick.**

- *100g mince*
- *1 Turkish or pita bread*
- *1tbs. satay sauce*
- *½ cup (50g) grated Mozzarella cheese*

Preheat oven to 180°C. Cook mince in a non-stick frypan and place aside. Place Turkish bread on a baking paper lined tray. Spread satay sauce over base, top with mince and sprinkle with cheese. Bake for 10 minutes or until cheese has browned.


# Sausage Rolls

**MAKES 2**

- *6 slices of bread*
- *2 tbs. (30g) butter*
- *3 thin pork sausages*

Preheat oven to 180°C. Remove crusts from bread and with a rolling pin roll bread until quite smooth. Boil sausages until partly cooked, approx. 6 minutes and allow to cool. Butter each slice of bread right to the edges, cut sausage in half and roll firmly in the bread, securing with two toothpicks. Cut in half and bake in oven on a foil lined tray until nicely browned.

# Savoury Butter

**MAKES ¼ CUP**

- 4 tbs. (60g) butter, softened
- 1 tbs. lemon juice
- Pinch celery salt
- Pinch cayenne pepper

Mix all ingredients together and serve.

# Savoury Cases

**The idea for the following stems from the clever Daphne Beutel.**

- 10 slices of bread
- 2 tbs. (30g) butter

Preheat oven to 180°C. Remove crusts and butter bread both sides. Press each slice into a muffin tray. Bake for 5 minutes or until golden.

*Optional: These may be cooled and stored in airtight containers until required. To reheat, simply place in hot oven for a few minutes.*

# Savoury Case Asparagus Filling

- 1 pkt white sauce
- 1½ cups (375ml) milk
- 200g tin asparagus pieces
- 1 lemon

Make the white sauce as per instructions using milk. Drain asparagus and mash with fork, then add to white sauce. Season with sea salt and pepper and serve in savoury cases topped with a generous amount of lemon zest.

# Savoury Case Curried Prawn Filling

- *1 pkt white sauce*
- *1½ cups (375ml) milk*
- *1 tps. curry powder*
- *12 medium green prawns*

Make the white sauce as per instructions using milk and then add curry powder. Chop prawns and add to the sauce, stir until prawns are orange in colour and cooked.


# Savoury Case Salmon Filling

- *1 pkt white sauce*
- *1½ cups (375ml) milk*
- *200g tin salmon*
- *1 tbs. finely chopped dill*

Make the white sauce as per instructions using milk. Drain salmon and mash with fork then add it and dill to the white sauce. Season with pepper.

# Sushi

- 1 cup (250g) of sushi rice or short grain rice
- 2 tbs. Japanese rice vinegar
- 2 sheets of Nori (or seaweed paper)
- ½ avocado

Preheat oven to 190°C. Wash rice and place into a casserole dish with 2 cups (500ml) of water, cover and cook for 25 minutes, set aside for 10 minutes, mix through vinegar.

Place some baking paper on a flat surface and lay a sheet of Nori (shiny side down) on top of it. Wet hands and spread a thin layer of rice evenly so you can still see 1 cm of Nori around circumference. Lay the avocado in the middle of the Nori going from one side to the other horizontally. Roll the sushi away from you keeping the roll firm. Damp the lip of the Nori before rolling it over fully and seal just as you would an envelope. Roll in cling film and leave to stand for 10 minutes before cutting so sushi sets.

*Optional: Can also use other fillings such as cucumber, asparagus, bean sprouts, shredded carrots, salmon, chicken, ginger, prawns, caviar. Serve with soy sauce and wasabi if you like.*

*Hint: Sushi is best served freshly made.*

# Sides

*Whatever you are, be a good one.*

Abraham Lincoln

---

# Salads

## Carrot, Sultana & Celery Salad

**SERVES 4**

- *4 carrots, peeled and grated*
- *1 cup (170g) sultanas*
- *1½ cups thinly sliced celery*
- *¼ cup (65g) whole egg mayonnaise*

Mix all ingredients together and chill before serving.

*Optional: Substitute celery for fresh pineapple.*


## Feta & Watermelon Salad

**SERVES 4**

- *½ watermelon*
- *2 tbs. mint leaves, finely chopped*
- *1 Spanish onion, finely chopped*
- *50g feta cheese*

Cut watermelon into chunky cubes and remove seeds. Add onion and mint and mix. When ready to serve drain excess juice and place in a serving bowl. Sprinkle with feta cheese.

*Optional: Serve with caramelised balsamic vinegar.*

---

# Feta & Beetroot Salad

**SERVES 4**

- *1 cup crumbled feta*
- *1 cup diced beetroot*
- *1 bag salad mix*
- *2 tbs. caramelised balsamic vinegar (see Salad Dressings).*

Combine first 3 ingredients and drizzle with the fourth.


# Garlic Pita Bread

**SERVES 4**

**This is a lighter option for use as a side dish instead of garlic bread.**

- *2 pita bread*
- *2 tsp. butter*
- *2 garlic cloves, crushed*

Preheat oven to 180°C. Mix butter with garlic and spread liberally over each pita bread. Cut into pie or wedge sized slices and place on lined baking tray. Bake for 10 minutes or until crisp.

# Mandarin Salad

**SERVES 4–6**

**Inspired by 'the best dancer ever' Neville McCosker.**

- ½ iceberg lettuce
- 3 mandarins, peeled
- 2 avocados, peeled and sliced
- 1 small Spanish onion, thinly sliced

Shred lettuce and add remaining ingredients. Cover and chill before serving with your favourite salad dressing.


# Octopus Salad

**SERVES 4**

- 1 kg baby octopus, cleaned
- ¾ cup (190ml) balsamic salad dressing
- 2 Lebanese cucumbers, diced
- 100g snow peas, trimmed

Place octopus and salad dressing in a bowl, marinate for at least 1hour. Preheat a non-stick frying pan until really hot. Cook undrained octopus in batches, turning frequently for 5 minutes until tender and slightly charred. Mount onto nests of cucumber and peas. Serve at once.

*Optional: If in your pantry, add ½ tsp. dried oregano to marinade.*

# Pasta Salad

**SERVES 6**

**A recipe by Kate Macdonald.**

- 500g pkt spinach pasta shells
- 190g jar basil pesto
- 1 small red onion, finely chopped
- ½ cup pine nuts, toasted

Cook the pasta according to packet directions. Once cooked, drain, rinse and allow to cool. Place in a serving bowl, mix through remaining ingredients and serve cold.


# Pea & Mint Salad

**SERVES 4**

- 2 cups fresh peas
- 2 tbs. fresh mint, chopped
- 1 cup crumbled feta cheese
- 2 tbs. fresh lemon juice

Place peas in a serving dish and allow to sit in boiling water for 2–3 minutes. Drain and rinse under cold water, allow to dry. Add mint and feta. Drizzle with juice and toss gently to combine.

# Pushkin's Salad

**SERVES 4**

**Recipe from 'Babushka' via Kent & Olya.**

- *4 carrots, grated*
- *2 cloves garlic, crushed*
- *½ cup (50g) walnuts, chopped*
- *4 tbs. mayonnaise*

Mix all ingredients together and serve. Substitute carrots for beetroots.

# Prawn & Mango Salad

**SERVES 4**

- *12 large peeled, de-veined and cooked prawns*
- *1 large mango, peeled and sliced*
- *1 cucumber, sliced finely*
- *1 cup (160g) roasted cashews, unsalted*

Mix all ingredients lightly and serve. Quick, easy and delicious!

# Rocket & Parmesan Salad

**SERVES 4**

**A recipe from the clever Cheyne McCorkindale.**

- *100g pkt rocket*
- *1–2 tbs. extra virgin olive oil*
- *½ Spanish onion, finely sliced*
- *25g parmesan cheese, finely grated*

Combine rocket and oil in a serving bowl. Add onions and parmesan and mix well, ensuring an even coating of parmesan across the rocket. Serve and enjoy!

# Spanish Orange Salad

**SERVES 4**

**A recipe from Jennette McCosker.**

- *½ iceberg lettuce*
- *2 oranges, peeled and sliced*
- *½ Spanish onion, thinly sliced*

Arrange lettuce on serving plate and top with sliced oranges and onions. Serve with your favourite salad dressing.

# Speedy Potato Salad

**SERVES 4–6**

**A recipe from Jan Neale.**

- *4 potatoes, washed and cubed*
- *4 bacon rashers, chopped and fried until crisp*
- *2 tbs. fresh mint, chopped*
- *¼ cup (60g) whole egg mayonnaise*

Boil potatoes until tender, approx. 6–8 minutes and allow to cool completely. Mix with remaining ingredients.

# Summer Salad

**SERVES 4**

**A little beauty created by Rachael to get Jaxson eating salad!!**

- *100g pkt mixed lettuce*
- *12 strawberries, washed*
- *60g snow peas, sliced*
- *2 fresh mangoes, sliced*

Wash all ingredients and drain excess water. Place lettuce into a serving bowl. Add hulled and quartered strawberries and snow peas. Remove skin from mango and slice flesh into the bowl. Squeeze juice from remaining mango and lightly toss throughout the salad. Serve and savour the flavour!

*Optional: Substitute sliced avocado for snow peas.*

# Tomato & Bocconcini Salad

**SERVES 4**

- *6 vine ripened tomatoes, sliced*
- *2 tbs. extra virgin olive oil*
- *4 bocconcini, thinly sliced*
- *½ cup fresh basil leaves*

Arrange tomato slices on a large flat serving plate, don't mind if they overlap. Drizzle with oil and top with slices of bocconcini and basil. Season generously with sea salt and pepper, cover and chill before serving.

*Optional: This salad is also lovely served with the zest of a lemon grated over it.*

*Hint: Basil leaves are best torn or used whole rather than cut with a knife as they bruise easily. As always, the herb is best used raw as cooking diminishes its flavour.*

# Potato

*You make a living by what you get. You make a life by what you give.*

Unknown

## Bacon Potatoes

**MAKES 1**

**A recipe from the lovely Katrina Price.**

- *1 large potato*
- *1 tbs. sour cream*
- *¼ tsp. Dijon mustard*
- *2 bacon rashers, chopped and lightly cooked*

Wrap potato in foil and bake in 180°C oven for approx. 1 hour or until cooked. Mix together sour cream, mustard and bacon. Scoop out 1–2 tbs. of potato and dollop in the mixture. Keep warm and serve as a meal or side dish.

## Chunky Skins

**SERVES 4**

- *3 large potatoes, washed and peeled thickly*
- *1 tbs. extra virgin olive oil*
- *Pinch of paprika*

Preheat oven to 200°C. Brush the potato skins with the oil and sprinkle with paprika. Bake for 20 minutes or until crunchy and golden brown. Serve either as a snack or with a main meal.

*Tip: Freeze the rest of the potato to use in another dish.*

# Crunchy Wedges

**SERVES 4**

**These are always a hit!**

- *2 large washed potatoes*
- *¼ cup (60ml) extra virgin olive oil*
- *2 cups (240g) cornflakes, crushed*
- *1 tbs. mixed herbs*

Preheat oven to 200°C. Cut potatoes into wedge shapes and place in large bowl. Drizzle olive oil until all wedges are covered. Coat generously with cornflakes and herbs. Place on flat baking tray. Cook for 20 minutes and then turn and cook for a further 15 minutes.

*Optional: Can also use sweet potato. Add parmesan cheese and paprika for an extra zing. Yum!!*

# Easy Potato Bake

**SERVES 6**

- *6 large potatoes, sliced thinly*
- *400g can condensed cream of mushroom soup*
- *½ cup (125ml) milk*
- *1 cup grated cheddar cheese*

Preheat oven to 180°C. Place potatoes into a casserole dish, combine soup and milk and pour over potatoes. Cover with cheese and bake in oven for 45 minutes or until potatoes are soft.

# Mashed Potato

**SERVES 4**

- 4 potatoes, peeled and cut
- 2 cloves garlic, crushed
- 1 tbs. extra virgin olive oil

Boil and mash potatoes until nice and smooth. Add garlic, oil and season with sea salt.


# Potato & Cheese Puffs

**SERVES 4**

- 2–3 cups cold mashed potato
- 2 free range eggs, separated
- 75g tasty cheese, grated

Preheat oven to 180°C. Combine potato with egg yolks and cheese, season with sea salt and pepper. Beat egg whites until stiff and fold into potato mixture. Drop tbs. of mixture onto a paper lined oven tray. Bake for 15–20 minutes until set and golden brown.

# Puffed Sweet Potato

**SERVES 4**

- 2 tbs. butter
- 2 cups mashed sweet potato
- ½ cup (125ml) milk
- 1 free range egg, separated

Preheat oven to 180°C. Melt 1 tbs. butter and to it add milk, season generously. Beat mixture into sweet potato, add yolk and mix well. Beat egg white until stiff peaks form and fold through mixture. Use 1 tbs. butter to grease a mini-muffin tray and dollop mixture into holes, bake in oven for 20–25 minutes or until nice and golden.

# Rosemary & Thyme Roast Spuds

**SERVES 6**

- 5 large scrubbed, peeled potatoes cut into thick wedges
- 4 tbs. extra virgin olive oil
- 8 sprigs fresh rosemary
- 8 sprigs fresh thyme

Preheat oven to 200°C. Toss spuds in oil and sprinkle with fresh herbs and some sea salt. Roast for 35–40 minutes, turning to evenly brown.

# Sliced Potato Cake

**SERVES 6**

- *4–5 potatoes, peeled and thinly sliced*
- *125g butter, melted*

Preheat oven to 200°C. Cover the base of a non-stick cake tin with potato slices and sprinkle with sea salt and pepper, brush with butter. Continue layers until potatoes are used. Cover tin with foil and bake for 45 minutes. Remove and let stand for 5 minutes. Cut into wedges before serving.


# Sweet Potato with Orange Glaze

**SERVES 6–8**

- *4 medium sweet potatoes*
- *½ cup (125ml) orange juice*
- *2 tbs. brown sugar*
- *1 tbs. cornflour*

Preheat oven to 180°C. Cut potatoes into thick slices then dry roast for 10 minutes or until just tender. In a saucepan, combine remaining ingredients with ½ cup water. Heat gently, stirring regularly until sauce has thickened. Place potato on a serving plate then cover with glaze, return to oven for 7 minutes. Garnish with orange rind.

*Hint: If you are not cooking sweet potato straight after peeling it, wrap it in foil to prevent it going black.*

# Scalloped Potatoes

**SERVES 4**

- 4 medium potatoes, peeled and sliced
- 1 pkt French onion soup
- 1½ cups (375ml) milk
- 2 tbs. (30g) butter, cubed

Preheat oven to 180°C. Place 1 layer of potatoes in a casserole dish and sprinkle with soup, repeat until you have used all the potatoes and soup mix. Pour over milk and top with butter cubes. Cover and cook for 1¼ hours or until potato is tender.


# Tasty Wedges

**SERVES 4**

- 4 washed potatoes
- 1 free range egg white, whisked
- 1 pkt spring onion or tomato soup
- 2 tbs. sunflower or macadamia nut oil

Preheat oven to 200°C. Cut potatoes into wedges. Brush with egg white, then sprinkle with your favourite soup mix. Place wedges on an oven tray and drizzle with oil. Cook in oven for 30 minutes or until crisp.

# Vegetables

*It's bizarre that the produce manager is more important to my children's health than the pediatrician.*

Meryl Streep

## Baked Spanish Onions

**SERVES 6–8**

- 4 large Spanish onions, sliced
- 4 slices multi-grain bread, grated into breadcrumbs
- 75g butter
- ½ cup (125ml) milk

Preheat oven to 150°C. Line a pie dish with breadcrumbs, then top with a layer of sliced onions. Season with sea salt and pepper and add several bits of butter. Add another layer of crumbs repeating the layering until the dish is full. Ensure last layer is crumbs. Pour milk over contents and bake for 1½ hours.

## Beans with Nutmeg

**SERVES 4**

- 250g beans
- 2 tbs. (30g) butter
- 1 tsp. nutmeg

Parboil beans for 1 minute then drain. Melt butter in frypan and add beans, season with nutmeg, toss over a low heat for 2–3 minutes.

# Brussel Sprout Bake

**SERVES 6**

**This is a lovely way to eat the good old Brussel Sprout!**

- *500g Brussel sprouts*
- *1 onion, chopped*
- *400g can condensed cream of celery soup*
- *1 cup grated tasty cheese*

Preheat oven to 180°C. Remember when cooking with Brussel sprouts to remove the tail and cut an X into the base to ensure heat penetrates the entire sprout. Cook the Brussel sprouts for about 3 minutes. Drain, cool slightly and cut into quarters. Mix with remaining ingredients (reserving 30g cheese) and place in a casserole dish, sprinkle reserved cheese on top. Bake for 20–30 minutes.

*Optional: Brussel sprouts can be substituted with cauliflower!*


# Bubble & Squeak

**SERVES 2**

- *1 cup mashed potato*
- *½ an onion, grated*
- *½ cup shredded cabbage*
- *¼ cup (60ml) olive oil*

Mix potato, onion and cabbage, season with sea salt and pepper and form into cakes. Shallow fry in hot oil until golden in colour.

*Optional: Add all other leftover vegetables (pumpkin, broccoli, corn etc) and gravy too, this moistens the mix making it 'bubble & squeak' as it cooks!*

# Cheese Topped Zucchinis (Courgettes)

**SERVES 2**

- 2 small zucchinis (courgettes)
- ⅓ cup grated cheddar cheese

In a saucepan, boil zucchinis until just tender. Drain and slice in half lengthways. Sprinkle with cheddar cheese and place under a hot grill until the cheese is golden brown.

# Garlic Spinach

**SERVES 4**

- 375g spinach, chopped
- 1tbs. (15g) butter
- 1 clove garlic, crushed

Cook spinach in small amount of salted water for 3 minutes, then drain. Heat butter in saucepan, add garlic and fry for 1 minute. Add spinach and cook stirring for 5 minutes. Season with sea salt and pepper.

# Gingered Carrots

**SERVES 4**

- 6 carrots, peeled and cut in half lengthways
- 2 tsp. fresh lemon juice
- ½ tsp. ground ginger
- 2tbs. (30g) butter

Preheat oven to 180°C. Place carrots in a baking dish. Mix lemon juice and ginger and season with sea salt and pepper, pour over carrots then dot with butter. Cover and bake for 45 minutes or until tender.

# Grilled Chilli Peaches/Nectarines

**SERVES 4**

**A recipe by Wendy King.**

- *8 ripe peaches or nectarines*
- *3½ tsp. sweet chilli sauce*

Preheat oven to 180°C. Cut fruit in half and remove stones. Drizzle a small amount of chilli sauce over each piece, flesh side up. Bake for 15 minutes to caramelise sweet chilli sauce and heat fruit through. Can also be cooked on a bbq.


# Herbed Zucchini (Courgette)

**SERVES 4**

- *3 zucchinis (courgettes), cut into thick diagonal slices*
- *1 tbs. (15g) butter*
- *1 tbs. finely chopped parsley*

Boil zucchinis for 3 minutes in salted water then drain well. Heat butter in non-stick frying pan, add zucchinis and season well. Sauté over low heat stirring occasionally until zucchinis are golden brown. Sprinkle with chopped parsley.

# Peas with Mint & Garlic Butter

**SERVES 4**

- *1 kg peas*
- *1 tbs. (15g) butter, chopped*
- *1 clove garlic, crushed*
- *⅓ cup (100g) small fresh mint leaves*

Cook the peas, drain and return to dry saucepan, add butter and garlic and season with sea salt and pepper. Gently toss before serving sprinkled with fresh mint leaves.


# Herb Roasted Mushrooms

**SERVES 6**

- *6 large field mushrooms*
- *1 tbs. mixed herbs*
- *1 tbs. (30g) butter*

Preheat oven to 170°C. Wash mushrooms and lay top side down onto a paper lined baking tray. Spread underside with butter and sprinkle with herbs. Roast for 20 minutes and serve.

# Snow Vegies

**SERVES 4**

- 4 cups of fresh vegetables of choice (peeled where necessary)
- 1 pkt white sauce mix
- 1½ cups (375ml) milk

Steam or slow boil vegetables. Mix white sauce to manufacturer's instructions using milk and pour over vegetables and serve.

*Optional: For variation, grate some orange zest into the white sauce.*


# Spinach with Lemon

**MAKES 4**

**This is a really nice way to each spinach!**

- 1 bunch fresh spinach, washed and shredded
- 2 tbs. (30g) butter, softened
- 2 tbs. lemon juice

Place spinach in saucepan of boiling water and boil for 5 minutes or until it has wilted., Drain well and return to dry saucepan, season with sea salt and pepper. Add butter and juice and toss together (a little lemon zest is nice too).

*Optional: Another delicious way to eat spinach is to sprinkle it with mint sauce.*

# Tomatoes with Feta Cheese

**MAKES 4**

**A recipe by the talented Janelle McCosker.**

- *4 vine ripened tomatoes*
- *200g feta cheese*
- *⅓ cup (80ml) pouring cream*
- *12 basil leaves*

Preheat oven to 180°C. Cut top off tomatoes, scoop out flesh. Blend cheese, cream and basil and season with sea salt and pepper. Refill tomatoes and replace lids. Place firmly in a shallow cake tin and bake in oven for 20 minutes.


# Vegetable Bake

**SERVES 4**

- *500g snap frozen vegetables, thawed and drained (or 2 big cups of fresh mixed vegetables)*
- *50g edam cheese, grated*
- *1 tsp. Paprika*

Place vegetables in an oven-proof dish, top with cheese and paprika. Grill until cheese lightly browns.

# Vegie Kebabs

**MAKES 8**

**The word 'kebab' is Arabic and means "on a skewer!"
Thanks Yo Yo Tippo!**

- *1 red pepper*
- *1 Spanish onion*
- *¼ fresh pineapple*
- *8 button mushrooms, washed*

Cut first 3 ingredients into chunks and thread alternately with mushrooms onto a soaked skewer. Grill on a hot bbq for a couple of minutes each side or until soft and warm.


# Zucchini (Courgette) Casserole

**Recipe by Gabrielle Bluett.**

- *1 tbs. extra virgin olive oil*
- *1 onion, diced*
- *3 zucchinis (courgettes), sliced*
- *1 tsp. dried oregano*

Mix all ingredients together. Place in a small casserole dish, cover and let marinate for 30 minutes in fridge. Preheat oven to 180°C and cook for 10 minutes.

# Zucchini (Courgette) Stir Fry

**SERVES 4**

- *2 tbs. (30g) butter*
- *6 zucchinis (courgettes), julienned*
- *25g parmesan cheese, grated*

Heat butter in frying pan and add zucchini. Cook on medium heat for 5 minutes, stirring frequently. Toss with sea salt and parmesan cheese just before serving.

# Mains

*When in doubt ... DON'T!.*

This applies to meat, men and mushrooms!!!

---

# Beef

## An Aussie Steak

**SERVES 2**

**Recipe by Rach's Dad, Billy Moore.**

- *2 beef steaks of choice*
- *2 tsp. vegemite*
- *1½ tbs. olive oil*

Spread 1 tsp. of vegemite over each steak and let marinate for ½ an hour. Heat the oil in a non-stick frying pan (or bbq), add steaks and cook to your liking.

# An English Steak

**SERVES 2**

**Recipe received by BBC Radio DJ.**

- *2 beef steaks of choice*
- *1 tsb. olive oil*
- *2 tbs. Branston Pickle*
- *40g stilton cheese*

Rub steaks with oil and grill until desired doneness. Remove and sit covered with foil for 4 mintues. Place steak on a paper lined baking tray, top with branston pickle and stilton and place under a grill for 2–3 minutes or until warmed through and cheese just starts to melt. Serve with your favourite vegetables.

# Bbq Beef Stir Fry

**SERVES 4**

**A little ripper Rachael created by accident in the middle of filming a cooking segment!!!**

- *½ kg lean cut beef strips*
- *3 tbs. sesame oil*
- *1 cup (250ml) bbq sauce*
- *1 red pepper, sliced thinly*

Marinate beef in bbq sauce for 4 hours or overnight in the fridge. Heat oil in a hot wok or frying pan. Add beef and cook on a hot temperature for 4 minutes then reduce heat. Add peppers, cover and simmer for 5 minutes. Serve immediately.

*Hint: Don't cook meat as it comes straight from the refrigerator. It is best restored to room temperature first to maximise tenderness.*

# Beef with Tangy Tomato Sauce

**SERVES 4**

- *½ kg beef strips*
- *½ cup (130g) tomato paste*
- *1 large onion, chopped*
- *250g sour cream*

In a non-stick frying pan brown beef. Add onion and simmer until cooked. Lastly add cream and tomato paste and season to taste. Mix well, serve over rice.

*Optional: Add a clove of crushed garlic when you add onion.*


# Beef & Potato Bake

**SERVES 4**

**A great way to use leftover meat and dinner is served!**

- *4 medium potatoes, cubed*
- *2½ cups cooked, chopped roast beef*
- *400ml can of condensed tomato soup*
- *2 cups grated tasty cheese*

Preheat oven 180°C. Combine first 3 ingredients and season. Pour into a casserole dish, bake covered for 1 hour or until potato is tender. Sprinkle with cheese and grill until cheese has melted.

# Beef Roma Pies

**MAKES 12**

**Simply sensational!**

- 4 sheets ready rolled puff pastry
- 500g lean mince
- 400g jar of your favourite pasta sauce
- 2 cups frozen peas, corn and peppers, thawed

Preheat oven to 200°C. In a non-stick frying pan brown mince, add vegies and season. Pour in sauce and simmer for 10 minutes. Whilst simmering, cut 6 large rounds into each sheet of pastry. Line a non-stick muffin tray with first 12 rounds, spoon in mince mix and top with final rounds of pastry. Seal with a fork. Bake for 20 minutes or until pastry is nice and golden.

# Blue Cheese Steaks

**SERVES 6**

- 6 rib eye steaks
- 200g stilton cheese
- 2 tbs. port
- 1 tbs. butter, melted

Cut a deep pocket through the side of each steak, try to keep the opening as small as possible. Mash the cheese and mix in the port. Stuff into pockets and close with damp toothpicks. Season steaks with pepper and brush with butter. Cook on bbq for about 3 minutes each side or until desired doneness.

# Carpetbag Snags

**SERVES 6**

- 1 kg thick beef sausages
- ½ cup (125ml) bbq sauce
- 12–18 oysters

Place sausages on a bbq and cook over medium heat until browned. Baste with sauce towards the end of cooking. Remove from heat and allow to cool slightly, slit sausages and place 2–3 oysters in each.

# Easy Casserole

**SERVES 4**

- 1 kg round steak, cubed
- 500g bag mixed frozen vegetables, thawed and drained (or 2 cups of fresh vegetables)
- 2 cups (500ml) vegetable juice

Preheat oven to 180°C. Place steak and vegetables in a casserole dish and pour over vegetable juice. Bake in oven for 1½ hours or until meat is nice and tender. Serve over rice to soak up the tasty sauce.

# Harch Steak

**SERVES 2**

**Recipe by Karen Harch.**

- *2 steaks of choice*
  *(eye fillet, rib fillet or lamb forequarters all work well)*
- *3 tbs. tomato sauce*
- *3 tbs. bbq sauce*
- *1 tbs. Worcestershire sauce*

Preheat oven to 190°C. Mix all liquid ingredients together. Place meat in a casserole dish and pour over the meat. Cover and cook for 1 hour (or until meat is cooked).

# Mustard Steak

**SERVES 2**

**Another ripper by Tony Van Dijk – perfect for the bbq!**

- *2 rib eye fillets*
- *2 tbs. seeded mustard*
- *2 tbs. extra virgin olive oil*
- *2 cups shredded lettuce*

Marinate steaks in mustard for 2–3 hours. Pan fry steak in a little olive oil for about 4 minutes on each side. Cut steaks across the grain and serve on a bed of lettuce.

# Rach's Mustard Roast Beef

**SERVES 4**

**This tastes absolutely incredible and is a delicious winter's evening meal!**

- *1 kg prime roasting beef*
- *4 tbs. seeded mustard*
- *5 tbs. macadamia nut oil or sunflower oil*

Preheat oven to 130°C. Line a baking dish with baking paper. Choose a dish just bigger than the size of the beef piece. Place beef in dish and glaze generously with mustard. Drizzle with oil and bake for 3 hours (cooking it for this time will ensure the beef is well done but still very tender). Turn beef at half way mark. Serve with your favourite roast vegies and gravy.

# Roast Beef

**SERVES 4**

**This is divine!**

- *1½ kg roast beef*
- *1 pkt French onion soup mix*
- *½ cup (125ml) red wine (any you would drink)*
- *⅓ cup (85ml) balsamic vinegar*

Place roast in the bottom of your slow cooker. Sprinkle with packet soup. Pour wine, vinegar and ½ cup of water over it. Cover and slow cook on low for approximately 6–7 hours ... That's it!

*Optional: When the roast is finished cooking, pour the liquids into a saucepan, heat on medium and add 2 tbs. cornflour that has been stirred into a little cool water for a really flavoursome gravy!*

# Shepherd's Pie

**SERVES 4**

**A recipe inspired from the Gippsland Harvest Festival, Victoria, Australia.**

- *500g lean mince*
- *1 cup (250g) fruit chutney*
- *6 potatoes, boiled and mashed*
- *75g tasty cheese, grated*

Preheat oven to 180°C. In a non-stick frying pan brown mince, season and mix through chutney. Pour into a casserole dish, top evenly with mashed potato and sprinkle with grated cheese. Bake in oven for 20–30 minutes or until cheese is nice and bubbly.

*Optional: Slice a tomato or two over the mince before topping with potato.*

# Silverside

**SERVES 6**

**A recipe from Jan Neale.**

- *1½ kg corned silverside*
- *1 tbs. vinegar*
- *1 tbs. golden syrup*
- *6 cloves*

Place silverside in a large saucepan, add enough water to just cover the meat. Stir through remaining ingredients. Bring to boil, then simmer, covered, for about 1½ hours or until tender.

# Simple Beef Stroganoff

**SERVES 4**

- *650g lean beef, cubed*
- *420g can condensed cream of mushroom soup*
- *200g button mushrooms*
- *250g sour cream*

Place beef cubes in slow cooker. Add soup and mushrooms. Cook on low for 6 hours. Stir in sour cream before serving and season to taste. Alternatively, brown meat in a saucepan over low heat, add remaining ingredients and simmer until sauce thickens and meat is cooked.

*Optional: Delicious served over rice or penne pasta.*

# Steak Burgundy

**SERVES 2**

**A favourite from Rach's butcher!**

- *2 good sized rib fillet steaks*
- *½ tbs. butter*
- *1 cup (250ml) red wine*
- *1½ tsp. finely crushed garlic*

Preheat oven to 180°C. Marinate steaks in red wine for 2 hours then place each steak in an envelope of foil ensuring you have plenty to twist the top over to seal. Mix butter and garlic together and place an equal dollop on top of each steak. Seal the steak in by folding over foil. Put on a baking tray and bake in oven for 45 minutes. YUM. YUM. YUM!

*Optional: Serve with roast vegetables or salad.*

# Steak with Mushroom Ragout

**SERVES 4**

**This is delicious!**

- *4 steaks*
- *2 tbs. butter*
- *250g mushrooms, sliced*
- *125ml double cream*

Brush steaks with half the butter. Preheat a frypan to hot. Cook first sides until moisture appears (approx. 3–4 minutes), turn and cook for another 3–4 minutes for medium doneness. Remove and cover with foil, allow to rest for 5 minutes. Meanwhile, place remaining butter and mushrooms in the frypan and cook until softened. Add cream and simmer until reduced and thickened (may need a little more cream). Season with sea salt and pepper.

*Optional: Serve with boiled potatoes and green beans.*

# Spicy Garlic Steak

**SERVES 2**

**Recipe by Paul Bermingham.**

- *1 garlic clove, finely chopped*
- *1 tsp. curry powder*
- *½ tsp. mixed herbs*
- *2 rib fillets*

Mix garlic, curry powder and mixed herbs together and coat the steak with the mixture. Place under a grill or on the bbq and cook to your liking. Let steak sit for 5 minutes before slicing thinly across the grain. Serve with salad.

# Spiced Corned Beef

**MAKES 6**

- 1½ kg corned silverside
- 1 orange, sliced
- ¼ cup (55g) brown sugar
- 1 cinnamon stick

Place corned beef in large saucepan. Add the orange, brown sugar and cinnamon stick. Just cover with water. Bring to the boil, cover and simmer for 1½ hours or until tender. Stand for 15 minutes before slicing.

*NB: A general rule of thumb for corned beef is to allow 30 minutes per 500g.*

*Optional: Serve with a dollop of mango chutney or tomato relish and roasted vegies.*


# Sweet Rissoles

**SERVES 4**

**Cheap, easy and delicious!**

- 400g can of corned beef
- ½ cup crushed pineapple, drained
- 1 cup mashed sweet potato
- 1 free range egg

Preheat oven to 180°C. Place all ingredients into a bowl and mix thoroughly. Roll into decent sized cakes and place onto a paper lined baking tray. Bake 30–40 minutes or until nicely browned. Can also do on a grill or bbq.

# Veal & Pesto Rolls

**SERVES 4**

**These are sensational.**

- *3 tbs. sun dried tomato pesto*
- *½ cup grated mozzarella*
- *4 veal schnitzels, flattened*
- *4 bacon rashers, rinds removed*

Combine pesto and cheese, fill schnitzels and season with sea salt and pepper. Roll firmly and wrap bacon around each, securing with either kitchen string or toothpicks. Cook in a non-stick frying pan, turning gently until cooked through.

# Zesty Meatballs

**MAKES 25**

- *500g extra lean mince*
- *⅓ cup (90g) tomato sauce*
- *⅓ cup (80ml) sherry*
- *2 tbs. brown sugar*

Preheat oven to 180°C. Season mince and using a tablespoon, shape into meatballs. Place meatballs on a foil lined baking tray and pop into oven for 30 minutes to brown. Remove and place into a casserole dish. Mix remaining ingredients and pour over meatballs. Bake for a further 30 minutes. Serve meatballs with sauce.

# Chicken

*The highest reward for a person's toil is not what they get for it, but what they become by it!*

John Ruskins

## Baked Chicken

**SERVES 6**

- *3 chicken breasts, halved*
- *⅔ cup (165g) natural yoghurt*
- *½ box savoury crackers (Ritz or similar), crushed*

Preheat oven to 180°C. Roll chicken in yoghurt and then in cracker crumbs. Place in a casserole dish and bake uncovered for 20 minutes, turn and bake a further 10 minutes.

*Optional: Delicious served with a nice, healthy salad.*

## Cheese & Ham Chicken Rolls

**SERVES 2**

- *2 chicken breast fillets*
- *1 tbs. seeded mustard*
- *2 pieces Swiss cheese*
- *2 pieces sliced ham*

Preheat oven to 180°C. Using a rolling pin, flatten chicken before smearing with mustard. Lay a piece of cheese followed by a piece of ham on each. Roll up and secure opening with a damp toothpick. Bake for 20 minutes or until brown and cooked through. Remove toothpick and cut into rounds to serve.

# Chicken Loaf

**SERVES 4**

**Enjoyed by the whole family.**

- *500g chicken mince*
- *1 cup (120g) seasoned stuffing mix*
- *2 free range eggs, beaten*
- *½ cup (130g) tomato paste*

Preheat oven to 180°C. Combine chicken, stuffing mix, eggs and half the amount of tomato paste. Shape into a log and place onto a paper lined baking tray. Spread remaining amount of tomato paste over the loaf. Bake in oven for 1 hour.

*Optional: Grate some vegies into this mix.*

*Hint: Place bacon in the bottom of your loaf dish when making a chicken or meatloaf. It not only adds flavour but your loaf will turn out easily without sticking.*

# Chicken Casserole

**SERVES 4**

**A recipe from Denise Bryant (via Kay Anderson).**

- *400g can condensed cream of chicken soup*
- *8 chicken pieces*
- *4 rashers bacon, chopped*
- *4 stalks celery, chopped*

Preheat oven to 180°C. Place chicken in a casserole dish topped with bacon and celery. Add soup and bake, uncovered, for 1¼ hours or until chicken is cooked.

# Chicken Sausages with Pesto Mash

**SERVES 4**

**A recipe from Brett McCosker.**

- *2 tbs. basil pesto*
- *4 large potatoes, cooked, drained and mashed*
- *8 chicken sausages*
- *Cranberry sauce to serve*

Add pesto to mashed potatoes and season to taste. Cook sausages in non-stick frying pan until cooked. Serve sausages with a dollop of cranberry sauce and mashed potato.

# Chicken with Lemon & Honey

**SERVES 6**

**A recipe from the lovely Cathy Dineen.**

- *1 chicken, cut into pieces*
- *2 lemons, quartered*
- *2 tbs. honey*
- *2 sprigs rosemary*

Preheat oven to 180°C. Put chicken skin side up in a large baking dish. Mix the juice of the lemons with the honey in a small bowl and pour over chicken pieces. Place squeezed lemon pieces in the baking dish for extra flavour. Season with sea salt and pepper. Cook for 45 minutes or until chicken is cooked and skin golden. Remove from oven and discard lemon halves. Pour juices into a saucepan and boil uncovered for about 5 minutes or until the juices have thickened slightly. Serve with rice or a salad.

# Chicken Wings with Curry Honey Glaze

**SERVES 6**

**A recipe from Kim Morrison.**

- *2 kg chicken wings*
- *½ cup (160g) honey*
- *1 tsp. curry powder*
- *2 tbs. soy sauce*

Place chicken wings in large dish. Combine remaining ingredients in a pan, heat until honey melts (add a little water if too thick). Pour over chicken wings. Marinate for several hours or refrigerate overnight. Bbq wings until cooked through. Baste frequently during cooking process.

# Curry Mayonnaise Chicken

**SERVES 2**

- ½ cup (130g) mayonnaise
- 1–2 tsp. curry powder
- 6 chicken legs
- 2 slices wholemeal bread, grated into breadcrumbs

Preheat oven to 180°C. Combine mayonnaise and curry, coat legs with the mixture. Roll in breadcrumbs and bake for 45–50 minutes or until cooked.

# Feta Chicken

**SERVES 2**

- 2 chicken breasts
- 250g feta cheese with basil and tomato (any flavour is nice)
- 3 tbs. olive oil
- ½ cup (65g) breadcrumbs

Preheat oven to 180°C. Gently mallet chicken until slightly thinner. Place 2 very generous strips of feta in the middle of a chicken breast and fold over, secure with a damp toothpick or two. Coat with oil and roll in breadcrumbs. Bake for 20 minutes or until meat is cooked. Allow to sit for 5 minutes before cutting into rounds before serving.

*Optional: Use seasoned stuffing mix instead of breadcrumbs.*

# Curried, Honey Mustard Chicken

**SERVES 4**

**Recipe by Cameron Hewitt. Quick, easy and ultra delicious!**

- *4 chicken breasts*
- *⅓ cup (100g) honey*
- *½–1 tsp. curry powder*
- *⅓ cup seeded mustard*

Preheat oven to 180°C. Cut the chicken into large strips. Mix honey, curry powder and mustard together. Coat the chicken with the mixture and place on paper lined baking tray. Bake for 25 minutes or until done.

# Magic Mango Chicken

**SERVES 4**

**Rachael created this little beauty by accident – little fat and tastes brilliant!!!!!!!**

- *3 tbs. sunflower oil*
- *2 chicken breasts, sliced into strips*
- *1 chicken stock cube dissolved in 1 cup of boiling water*
- *1 fresh mango, peeled and sliced*

Heat oil in a wok or frying pan. Add chicken and fry till golden brown. Reduce heat and add stock and the mango slices. Simmer for around 15 minutes and serve.

*Optional: Serve with rice and a few of your favourite vegies.*

# Orange Roast Chicken

**SERVES 4**

**Recipe by Carly Nelson, a beauty for Sunday roasts or even on the table at Christmas time!**

- *1 large uncooked chicken*
- *½ cup (125ml) sunflower oil*
- *2 oranges*
- *1 tbs. fresh mixed herbs*

Preheat oven to 180°C. Place chicken in a baking paper lined roasting tray breast side up. Drizzle with oil. Grate the skin of one of the oranges and juice both oranges over the chicken. Finally sprinkle herbs, cover with foil and roast chicken for 1½ hours or until cooked to your liking (remove foil in final half hour). Remove from oven and allow to rest for 5 minutes before cutting and serving.

*Hint: It usually takes 30 minutes per 500g of weight to cook a chicken in a preheated oven at 180°C.*


# Roma Chicken

**SERVES 4**

**A super tasty recipe from Katrina Price.**

- *½ a roast chicken, remove skin*
- *400ml bottle of your favourite tomato based pasta sauce*
- *1 red pepper, de-seeded and sliced*
- *2 tbs. sour cream*

Cut up chicken, mix with pasta sauce and peppers in a non-stick frying pan. Season to taste. Bring to the boil. Reduce heat and simmer for 5 minutes. Just before serving, stir in sour cream.

*Optional: Serve over rice or penne pasta.*

# Swiss Schnitzel

**SERVES 4**

**A fabulous recipe from the lovely Lynette Willson.**

- *2 chicken breasts*
- *3 slices of multigrain bread, grated into crumbs*
- *2 tbs. extra virgin olive oil*
- *4 slices Jarlsberg cheese*

Cut chicken in half, then using a rolling pin or mallet pound slices until thin. Coat with breadcrumbs, pressing into flesh to coat both sides. Heat oil in a large non-stick frying pan. Over moderate heat cook schnitzels 2 at a time for 2 minutes, until golden on the bottom, turn and top with cheese. Cook for a further 3 minutes or until chicken is tender and the cheese melts.

*Optional: Pop under a hot grill just at the end.*

# Tangy Chicken Tenderloins

**SERVES 4**

- *3 chicken breasts, sliced*
- *3 tbs. flour*
- *1 cup (280g) bbq sauce*
- *½ cup (125ml) orange juice*

Preheat oven to 180°C. Coat chicken with flour. Brown in a non-stick pan and place in a shallow baking pan. Mix bbq sauce and orange juice and pour over chicken. Bake covered for 10 minutes. Remove from oven, spoon sauce over chicken and bake uncovered for another 10–15 minutes or until done.

# Yummy Drummies

**SERVES 4**

- *4 tbs. honey*
- *2 tbs. soy sauce*
- *2 tbs. lemon juice*
- *8 chicken drumsticks, skinned*

Blend honey, soy sauce and lemon juice together to make a marinade. Place chicken in a casserole dish and pour marinade over the top of each piece. Cover and refrigerate for 2 hours. Preheat oven to 220°C and cook chicken for around 40–50 minutes or until cooked throughout. Serve with vegetable of choice.

# Fish

*Life is a journey that is homeward bound.*

Anonymous

---

## Almond Fish Fillets

**SERVES 4**

**Paul Bermingham's little beauty that the kids just love.**

- *8 pieces white fish fillets*
- *1 cup (260g) organic mayonnaise*
- *1 cup (175g) plain flour*
- *1½ cups (240g) slivered almonds*

Preheat oven to 180°C. Coat fillets with mayonnaise. Combine flour and almonds and roll fillets in dry ingredients. Place on a lined baking tray and bake for 10–15 minutes or until fish flakes easily.

*Optional: Serve with summer salad when it's hot or with yummy green vegies in winter. You can also substitute this with chicken and it works beautifully — you just need to cook for 10 minutes longer.*

# Apricot Fish

**SERVES 4**

**Yummy!**

- *500g fresh white fish fillets*
- *3 tbs. fresh lemon juice*
- *⅓ cup (80g) natural yoghurt*
- *3 tbs. apricot jam*

Preheat oven to 180°C. Place lemon juice in a baking dish with fish. Bake uncovered for 5 minutes then drain. Meanwhile, combine remaining ingredients and spoon over fish. Return to oven for a further 5 minutes or until cooked.


# Baked Fish

**SERVES 2**

- *2 fresh white fish fillets*
- *1 tsp. butter, melted*
- *1 lemon*

Preheat oven to 180°C. Coat fish with butter and season with sea salt and pepper. Cut lemon and place slices on fish. Wrap fish in foil. Cook in oven for 10–15 minutes or until fish is tender (depending on thickness).

*Optional: Can sprinkle a little garlic or herbs on fish before wrapping.*

# Cheesy Fish Steaks

**SERVES 4**

- 4 fish steaks
- 90g cheddar cheese, grated
- 1 tsp. Worcestershire sauce
- 1 tbs. milk

Place fish steaks under a 160°C grill for 5 minutes. Mix remaining ingredients and season with sea salt and pepper. Turn the fish and spread the uncooked side with cheese mix. Grill for a further 5 minutes or until fish is cooked and the topping bubbling.

*Optional: Garnish with fresh chopped parsley, also nice made with salmon steaks.*


# Dukkah Crusted Salmon

**SERVES 4**

**This is absolutely delish ...**

- 4 skinless salmon fillets
- Olive oil spray
- ⅓ cup (40g) dukkah

Preheat oven to 150°C. Place salmon on a foil lined baking tray. Lightly spray each fillet with oil, then press dukkah onto both sides of each fillet. Bake for 10–15 minutes or to your liking.

# Easy Salmon Rissoles

**SERVES 4**

**A recipe from Marie McColl ... Quick, easy & delicious!**

- *400g can pink salmon*
- *½ cup (130g) whole-egg mayonnaise*
- *1 cup mashed potato*
- *1 cup crushed Ritz crackers*

Preheat oven to 120°C. Mix all ingredients together and season with pepper. Shape into cakes and bake for 20 minutes or until golden.

*Optional: Pan fry for 4 minutes each side or until golden.*


# Lemon Fish

**SERVES 4**

- *4 fish fillets*
- *1 tbs. butter*
- *1 lemon, juiced*
- *2 tbs. freshly chopped parsley*

Season fish with pepper. Place under grill. Mix butter, juice and ½ tsp. rind together and spread over fish. Grill until lightly browned. Turn carefully then spread with remaining lemon mix. Grill until cooked. Serve garnished with lemon slices and parsley.

*Hint: Often a nice accompaniment to fish is a glass of water with ice cubes that have been frozen with little slices of lemon in them.*

# Lime & Salmon Cakes

**SERVES 6**

**Y.U.M.M.Y!**

- *1 lime*
- *400g can pink salmon, drained*
- *1 free range egg*
- *3 slices wholemeal bread, grated into crumbs*

Grate lime zest, then juice the lime. Place zest, juice and remaining ingredients in a bowl, season with pepper. Mix well before shaping into 12 thick cakes. Cook in a greased non-stick pan until heated through.

*Hint: Fresh bread is easier to grate when frozen.*


# Salmon Delight

**SERVES 4**

**A recipe from the vibrant Katrina Price.**

- *4 salmon steaks, skinless*
- *4 slices prosciutto*
- *12 cherry tomatoes*
- *200g green beans, top 'n' tailed*

Preheat oven to 180°C. Wrap the salmon steaks in prosciutto and place in a baking dish. Add the cherry tomatoes and beans. Bake for 10–15 minutes.

*Optional: Serve with lemon wedges.*

# Salmon Mornay

**SERVES 4**

- 400g can pink salmon, drained
- 2 tsp. lemon juice
- 400g can condensed cream of celery soup
- 60g grated cheese

Preheat oven to 190°C. Combine salmon, juice and soup, season with cracked pepper. Place in an oven proof dish, top with cheese and bake for 30 minutes.

*Optional: Add some chopped onion or celery if you have.*


# Salmon Wellington

**SERVES 4**

**A recipe from the lovely Wendy Beattie, great for a dinner party!**

- 4 salmon steaks, skin off
- 2 sheets ready rolled puff pastry
- 8 cherry tomatoes
- 2 tbs. basil pesto

Preheat oven to 180°C. Cut ready rolled puff pastry sheets in half and smooth ½ tbs. of pesto down the middle of each half. Place salmon on top of pesto and slice cherry tomatoes on top of salmon. Season if you like. Roll pastry over salmon ensuring all edges are sealed. Cook for 30 minutes or until golden brown.

*Optional: Before sealing, drizzle with freshly squeezed lemon juice. For added effect, sprinkle sesame seeds on top before baking.*

# Salsa Surprise Fish

**SERVES 4**

**This will surprise and delight!**

- 4 fresh white fish fillets
- ½ cup (90g) thick and chunky salsa
- 2 tbs. honey
- 2 tbs. Dijon mustard

Preheat oven to 180°C. Place fish in a paper lined baking dish. Bake in oven uncovered for 5 minutes, then drain. Meanwhile, combine remaining ingredients and pour over fish. Return to oven for 5 minutes or until fish is cooked and sauce is heated through.


# Swiss Fish

**SERVES 4**

- 2 tbs. (30g) butter
- 4 fresh white fish fillets
- 4 slices Swiss cheese
- 1 ripe avocado

Preheat oven to 180°C. Melt butter in a non-stick frypan on medium heat. Add fish fillets, cooking on 1 side for approx. 2 minutes before flipping (cooking time is dependent on how thick the fish fillet is). Lay cooked fillets on a tray lined with baking paper and top with Swiss cheese. Melt in oven for about 5 minutes and then top with a sliver or two of avocado and serve with salad.

# Tarragon Fish

**SERVES 4**

- *4 fresh white fish fillets*
- *½ cup (125g) natural yoghurt*
- *1 tsp. dried tarragon*
- *2 tbs. grated tasty cheese*

Preheat oven to 180°C. Place fish in a greased baking dish. Bake in oven uncovered for 5 minutes, then drain. Meanwhile, combine remaining ingredients and spread over fish. Return to oven for 3–5 minutes or until cheese has melted.


# Tuna & Tomato Risotto

**SERVES 4**

**A recipe from the talented Marie McColl.**

- *5 cups (1.25 ltr) seafood or vegetable stock*
- *2 cups (370g) arborio rice*
- *400g can flaked tuna in brine, drained*
- *400g can chopped tomatoes*

Bring stock to boil, add rice and reduce heat and simmer for 20 minutes Add tuna and tomatoes, season to taste. Continue to simmer, stirring regularly, until all liquid has absorbed. Then serve.

# Lamb

*Laughter is brightest where food is best.*

Irish Proverb

---

## Asian Bbq Lamb Chops

**SERVES 4**

- *8 lamb chops*
- *3 tsp. soy sauce*
- *3 tbs. sweet chilli sauce*

Mix soy and sweet chilli sauces. Cook chops on bbq for 1–2 minutes each side. Reduce heat and continue cooking for 2–3 minutes while brushing with baste. Cover loosely with foil and rest for 5 minutes before serving.

## Balsamic Glazed Lamb Cutlets

**SERVES 4**

**This is an absolute WINNER!**

- *12 lamb cutlets*
- *1 tbs. balsamic vinegar*
- *1 tbs. honey*
- *2 tbs. fresh rosemary leaves*

Heat frypan, grill or bbq. Mix last 3 ingredients. Cook cutlets for 1–2 minutes each side or until just starting to brown. Brush with baste and cook a further 3 minutes each side, basting occasionally. Serve drizzled with the tasty jus.

# Chilli Lamb Rissoles

**MAKES 8**

- *500g lamb mince*
- *1 free range egg, lightly beaten*
- *1 cup (100g) rolled oats*
- *¼ cup (80g) sweet chilli sauce*

Combine all ingredients together in a bowl and season with sea salt and pepper. Form into rissoles, heat a non-stick pan or greased bbq plate, and cook turning occasionally for 15 minutes or until cooked through depending on size.

# Chinese-Style Lamb Roast

**SERVES 4–6**

**Try it ... You'll be surprised!**

- *1½ kg lamb roast*
- *375ml can evaporated milk*
- *½ cup (140g) hoisin or teriyaki sauce*

Preheat oven to 180°C. Place the lamb into an oven bag. Combine the milk and sauce. Pour about half over the lamb (remaining can be frozen for another time) and tightly seal the bag, piercing a few holes around the end. Roast the lamb for 1½ hours or until desired doneness. Serve with fried rice.

*Optional: Garnish with fresh coriander.*

*Hint: To maintain freshness of coriander; wrap it in a damp tea towel and refrigerate.*

# Curry Lamb Pies

**MAKES 8**

**Great in winter!**

- *4 slices of wholemeal bread, remove crusts and flatten slightly*
- *1 tbs. (15g) butter*
- *400g can lamb curry*

Preheat oven to 180°C. Butter bread both sides. Using a scone cutter, cut rounds from bread and press into fairy cake tin. Bake for 5 minutes or until golden brown. Heat lamb curry and spoon into cases.

# Glazed Lamb Chops

**SERVES 4–6**

- *4–6 lamb loin chops, about 2cm thick*
- *⅓ cup (100g) orange marmalade*
- *2 tbs. lemon juice*

Place lamb under a grill for 6 minutes, season and turn. Grill the other side for 5 minutes, or until almost cooked to desired doneness. Season second side. Combine the marmalade and lemon juice, spread evenly over the lamb chops and grill for about 2 minutes longer.

# Irish Stew

**SERVES 4–6**

**This is YUMMY!!**

- *1 kg lamb neck chops*
- *3 large onions, sliced*
- *1 kg potatoes, peeled and sliced*
- *2 tbs. Worcestershire sauce*

Preheat oven to 160°C. Arrange a layer of chops in a casserole dish. Season with sea salt and pepper. Cover with a layer of onions and then potatoes. Repeat until all used. Sprinkle sauce over the top, then pour in enough water to come two-thirds up the dish. Place on cook top and bring to the boil. Cover and bake for 2½ hours.

*Optional: Can use beef stock instead of water. Add whatever vegies you have in the fridge.*

# Lamb Rissoles

**MAKES 8**

- *500g lamb mince*
- *1 onion grated*
- *2 tbs. mint jelly*

Preheat oven to 180°C. Combine all ingredients and season with sea salt and pepper. Form into rissoles and bake in moderate oven for 20 minutes or until cooked through.

*Optional: These are also fine to pan-fry and are delicious served with a dollop of Raita.*

# Lamb Samosas

**MAKES 12**

- 500g lamb mince
- ½ a 283g can Tikka Masala (medium) – remainder can be frozen for later
- 2 tbs. (30g) butter
- 12 filo pastry sheets

Preheat oven to 190°C. Fry mince in a non-stick frying pan until brown. Add curry and cook a further 2 minutes then set aside. Melt remaining butter, cut pastry sheets in half lengthways. Brush one strip of pastry with butter, then lay another strip on top and brush again. Place a generous spoonful of lamb in the corner of the strip and fold over to form a triangular package, continue to fold. Brush with butter and place on a baking sheet. Repeat using the remaining ingredients. Bake for 15–20 minutes until golden. Serve hot.

*Optional: These are DELICIOUS served with sweet chilli sauce and are a real hit made smaller as a nibble when friends and family gather!*

# Moroccan Spiced Lamb

**SERVES 2**

**A recipe from the lovely Lisa Darr.**

- *2 lamb backstraps*
- *1 tbs. extra virgin olive oil*
- *2 tsp. Moroccan spice*

Preheat oven to 220°C. Rub flesh of lamb with oil, then coat well with the spice. Place on a baking tray and roast for 15 minutes for medium or until cooked to your liking. Remove lamb, cover with foil and rest for 10 minutes before serving.

*Optional: According to Chef, Peter Wolf from the Eumundi Markets in Queensland, Australia. To cook on a bbq simply heat grill to hot and for well done cook 4 minutes each side, for medium 3 minutes, and rare 2 minutes.*


# Pesto Lamb

**SERVES 2**

**A great little creation of Rachael's inspired by her local butcher!**

- *4 lamb cutlets*
- *2 tbs. basil pesto*
- *1 tsp. finely grated lemon rind*
- *1 tbs.(15g) butter*

Preheat oven to 180°C. Combine basil pesto, lemon rind and butter. Place each cutlet in an envelope of foil and dollop a tbs. of mixture on top of all the cutlets. Fold the foil to seal firmly and cook for 30 minutes.

*Optional: Substitute basil pesto and lemon rind with 4 tbs. garlic flavoured pasta sauce and some parmesan cheese.*

# Prosciutto & Pesto Cutlets

**SERVES 4**

**A beauty from Brian Neale, Byron Bay NSW.**

- 8 lamb cutlets
- ¼ cup (65g) basil pesto
- 4 slices prosciutto

Spread cutlets with pesto. Wrap with prosciutto. Grill each side until cutlets are cooked. Simply delicious served with a salad.

# Roast Lamb

**SERVES 4**

- 1½ kg leg of lamb
- 2 tbs. extra virgin olive oil
- 1 tbs. seeded mustard
- 2 tbs. honey

Preheat oven to 180°C. Use a knife to make small cuts in the meat, rub with oil. Mix mustard and honey together and baste the meat, rubbing the mixture into the cuts. Bake for 1½ hours for rare to medium or 2 hours for medium to well done.

*Optional: Press fresh rosemary twigs into the cuts.*

*Hint #1: With any roast lamb, the flavour can be enhanced by making tiny slits in the meat and filling them with fresh mint before roasting. Or simply baste with yoghurt or orange juice during cooking.*

*Hint #2: When cooking a roast, instead of oil place water in the baking pan.*

# Pasta

*Minds are like parachutes, they only function when open.*

Thomas Dewar

---

## Chorizo Gnocchi

**SERVES 4**

- *1 small red onion, diced*
- *2 chorizo sausages, thinly sliced*
- *1 pkt. fresh potato gnocchi, cooked and drained*
- *575g jar Napolitana pasta sauce*

Cook onion and chorizo together in a large non-stick pan for 3 minutes or until golden. Add gnocchi, sauce and ¼ cup (60ml) water. Season with sea salt and pepper. Simmer for 20 minutes or until heated through.

*Optional: Top with freshly grated parmesan to serve.*

# Creamy Pasta Sauce

**SERVES 4**

**A recipe from Jan Neale.**

- 4 salad onion tops, finely chopped
- 4 rashers bacon, chopped
- 200g button mushrooms, sliced
- 200g cream cheese, softened

Combine salad onion tops and bacon in large fying pan, stir until bacon is crisp. Add mushrooms, stir until softened. Add cream cheese and a third a cup of boiling water, simmer until cream cheese has melted.

# Creamy Pesto Chicken Gnocchi

**SERVES 4**

- 300ml cream
- ¼ cup (65g) basil pesto
- 500g coarsely chopped, cooked chicken
- 500g gnocchi

Simmer cream and pesto in a frying pan for 5 minutes. Add chicken and gnocchi, mix well and serve warm.

*Optional: Sprinkle with basil leaves or parmesan cheese.*

# Easy Macaroni Cheese

**SERVES 4**

**A recipe by Michelle Dodd.**

- *400g macaroni*
- *⅓ cup (80ml) pouring cream*
- *1¼ cup (300ml) milk*
- *150g cheddar cheese, grated*

Cook the macaroni in a large saucepan of boiling water for 6 minutes or until al dente. Drain and return to the saucepan. Add the cream, milk and cheese to the pan, stir over a low heat until the cheese melts and the mixture is thick and coats the pasta.

# Fettuccine Alfredo

**SERVES 4**

**This is sensational!**

- *4 tbs. (60g) butter*
- *1 cup (250ml) double cream*
- *90g parmesan cheese, grated*
- *400g fresh fettuccine*

While boiling pasta, melt butter in a large fry pan and add cream bringing it to the boil. Simmer for 5 minutes, stirring constantly, add ¾ of the cheese and season well. Reduce heat, add drained (not rinsed) pasta and toss until thoroughly coated. Serve sprinkled with remaining Parmesan.

# Fettuccine Chicken

**SERVES 4**

**A tasty pasta dish from Nikki Goodwin.**

- *450g pkt fettuccine*
- *250g cooked chicken*
- *400g can cream of condensed chicken soup*

Cook fettuccine to manufacturer's instructions. Drain excess water and add chicken and soup, stir to heat throughout and serve.

*Optional: Sprinkle with some grated cheese or add some quartered snow peas or vegetable of choice.*

*Tip: This is a great way to use any leftover roast chicken.*


# Macaroni Bake

**SERVES 4**

**A recipe from the wonderful Jenny Postle.**

- *4 cups cooked macaroni (approx. 2 cups uncooked)*
- *400g can tomato soup*
- *250g diced ham or bacon*
- *1 cup grated cheddar cheese*

Preheat oven to 180°C. Place macaroni, soup and ham in a bowl and mix well before pouring into a casserole dish. Top with grated cheese and bake in oven for 20 minutes.

*Optional: Mix some freshly grated breadcrumbs into the cheese topping.*

# Mary's Spaghetti Sauce

**SERVES 2**

- *1 onion, sliced finely*
- *2 bacon rashers, sliced finely*
- *400g lean mince*
- *400g can of condensed tomato soup*

In a fry pan sauté onion. Add bacon and cook until brown. Add mince and cook to your liking. Add enough soup to create a thickened consistency and serve.

*Optional: This is a stand-alone recipe or you can serve it with your favourite pasta or on some toast. Quick and easy and very tasty.*


# Pasta & Broccoli

**SERVES 4**

**A southern Calabrese Italian recipe from Peter Paladino.**

- *400g pkt spaghetti*
- *⅓ cup (80ml) cup extra virgin olive oil*
- *2 cloves garlic, crushed*
- *3 heads of broccoli*

Bring 3 ltr. of salted water to the boil. Add broccoli and simmer. When half cooked, add pasta, cooking according to packet instructions. Strain pasta and broccoli into a colander. In the cooking pot, heat the oil and garlic over a medium heat for 1–2 minutes. Return pasta and broccoli to the pot stirring to combine.

*NB: The broccoli should be well broken down and little bits stuck to each strand of pasta.*

*Optional: Serve with grated parmesan if you like.*

# Pesto Pasta

**SERVES 4**

- 400g linguine
- 190g jar basil pesto
- 1 punnet grape or cherry tomatoes, cut in half
- 100g parmesan cheese, grated

Cook pasta as per instructions. Stir in ½ the basil pesto, adding more if required. Toss gently over low heat until pasta is coated. Add grape tomatoes and toss for 1 minute. Sprinkle with cheese and serve.

*Optional: Roast seasoned tomatoes in a 180°C oven for 5 minutes first.*


# Pinenut Pasta

**SERVES 2**

**Recipe by forever NSW loyal Lea 'Boof' Van Dijk.**

- ¾ cup (120g) pinenuts
- 1 tbs. (15g) butter
- 200g spinach fettucine
- 45g parmesan cheese, grated

Put butter and pinenuts in a warm fry pan and cook until golden brown. Bring a saucepan of water to the boil and cook pasta to packet instructions. Drain water and toss pasta with pinenuts and parmesan.

*Optional: A little cracked pepper tastes great too.*

# Prosciutto Pasta

**SERVES 2**

- *3 slices prosciutto*
- *200g thin spaghetti*
- *2 tbs. (30ml) extra virgin olive oil*
- *100g parmesan cheese, grated*

Bring a saucepan of water to the boil and cook pasta to packet instructions. Thinly slice prosciutto and mix with parmesan cheese. Drain pasta and add the oil. Stir in prosciutto and cheese and serve.

*Optional: Top with a little parsley.*

# Pork

*As a child my family's menu consisted of two choices: Take it or leave it!*

Buddy Hackett

---

## A Pie for A Guy

**SERVES 4**

**A recipe from Shane Hunia, Coromandel New Zealand.**

- *2 sheets ready rolled puff pastry, thawed*
- *½ an onion, diced*
- *4 bacon rashers, roughly chopped*
- *6 free range eggs*

Preheat oven to 200°C. Place first sheet of ready rolled puff pastry in a medium sized paper lined quiche dish. Cover the base with onion and then bacon. Crack each egg (without breaking the yolk) spanning the entire base. Season generously with sea salt and pepper before topping with final sheet of pastry. Using a fork, seal the edges and trim excess pastry. Pierce the lid 4 times and bake in oven for 25 minutes.

# Bacon & Cannellini Risotto

**SERVES 4**

**This is S.C.R.U.M.P.T.I.O.U.S!**

- *4 bacon rashers, roughly chopped*
- *1.25 ltr chicken stock*
- *2 cups (370g) arborio rice*
- *400g can cannellini beans*

Whilst frying bacon in a large non-stick frying pan, bring stock to boil in a saucepan. Add rice to frying pan with bacon and stir to coat, add stock, reduce heat, cover and simmer for 20 minutes. Add beans, season with sea salt and pepper. Continue to simmer until rice is soft and stock has been fully absorbed.

*Optional: Replace cannellini beans with peas.*

# Easy Pork Bites

**MAKES 36**

**A recipe from the brilliant Michelle Dodd ... Soooooooo easy!**

- *6 flavoured sausages eg. Italian, herb and garlic, honey and rosemary,rosemary and lamb ... Whatever takes your fancy!*

Preheat oven to 180°C. Squeeze the contents of sausages into a bowl. Roll into bite-sized balls, place on a foil lined baking tray and bake in oven for 10 minutes or until cooked. Serve warm with your favourite dipping sauce.

# Country Bbq Pork Ribs

**SERVES 4**

- *1 kg pork ribs*
- *2 large onions, sliced*
- *1 clove garlic, crushed*
- *300ml bottle of smokey bbq sauce*

Place ribs in bottom of slow cooker. Add onions, garlic, and sauce. Cover and cook on low for 7–8 hours.

# Ham on the Bone

**SERVES 8**

**A recipe by the funky Franj Oberman.**

- *⅓ cup (80g) brown sugar*
- *1 cup (320g) apricot jam*
- *1½ kg leg of ham*
- *¼ cup cloves*

Preheat oven to 150°C. Place brown sugar and jam in a saucepan and dissolve. Remove outer skin of ham and score creatively with a sharp knife. Place cloves in scored corners then glaze. Cook for an hour or until "you like what you see." Carve and serve.

*Glaze Options:*

- *2 cups brown sugar, ½ cup honey, juice from one can of pineapple rings. Mix until smooth and spoon half over the ham, applying remainder half way through baking. Use pineapple rings to garnish.*
- *Cloves and honey*
- *English mustard and demerara sugar*
- *3 pineapple rings, ½ a can of pineapple juice and 1 tbs. honey. Put all ingredients into a blender ... Then cook in a small saucepan until desired thickness.*

# Glazed Pork Tenderloins

**SERVES 4**

**A recipe from the bright and bubbly Julie McDonald OAM.**

- *2 pork tenderloins (approx. 500g)*
- *⅓ cup (80ml) salt reduced soy sauce*
- *2 tbs. honey*
- *2 tbs. Worcestershire sauce*

Preheat oven to 160°C. Trim the tenderloins of excess fat. Combine the soy, honey and Worcestershire sauce in a shallow dish with the tenderloins. Cover and refrigerate overnight, turning several times. Grill the pork over a medium grill for about 20 minutes or to prepare in the oven, bake for about 50 minutes, basting periodically.

# Perfect Pork Roast with Crackling

**SERVES 4–6**

- *1 kg pork loin, scored*
- *3 large sprigs rosemary*

Preheat oven to 220°C. Place pork on a cake rack in a baking dish, skin side down. Pour enough water into dish so as not to touch the pork and add rosemary. Bake for 20 minutes. Turn pork so skin is facing up, sprinkle with 2 tbs. of sea salt and bake for further 20 minutes. Reduce heat to 180°C and cook for a further 20 minutes. Allow to rest for 20 minutes before slicing.

# Pork & Asparagus Casserole

**SERVES 4**

- *400g condensed cream of asparagus soup*
- *2 granny smith apples*
- *4 pork chops, trimmed of fat*

Peel and slice apples. Put can of soup, apple and pork in saucepan. Simmer until pork is tender (approx. 1 hour).

*Optional: Add some sultanas and serve with your favourite roast vegies.*


# Pork Fillets with Dried Fruit

**SERVES 2**

**These are d.e.l.i.c.i.o.u.s!**

- *2 pork fillets*
- *1 cup (170g) dried mixed fruit*
- *½ onion, finely chopped*
- *2 rashers bacon*

Preheat oven to 180°C. Soak fruit in boiling water for 10 minutes or until plump and soft, then drain. Cut a lengthways slit ¾ way through each fillet. Fry onion until brown and mix with fruit. Press into each fillet, wrap in bacon and tie with string. Seal all over in hot pan, then bake in oven for 20 minutes.

# Pork & Pumpkin Curry

**SERVES 4**

- *½ kg pork, cubed*
- *½ kg pumpkin, cubed*
- *2 tbs. red curry paste*
- *400g tin coconut cream*

Over medium heat, brown pork in a large saucepan, add curry paste and stir, cooking for 5 minutes. Pour cream into pan, add ½ cup (125ml) water and pumpkin, season to taste and bring to the boil. Reduce heat and simmer for 30–40 minutes or until the pork is cooked.

*Optional: This is best made a few hours prior to serving as it thickens as it cools. Simply reheat when ready to serve.*


# Pork Roll

**SERVES 4**

- *500g pork sausages*
- *1 free range egg*
- *1 onion, grated*
- *1 cup (130g) fresh breadcrumbs*

Preheat oven to 180°C. Cut away skin from sausages. Mix pork, egg and onion together and season with sea salt and pepper. Form into a loaf and roll in breadcrumbs. Place in a baking dish and bake in oven turning after 20 minutes. Then cook for a further 20 minutes.

*Optional: Serve bathed in apple sauce ... Surprisingly yummy!*

# Sausage Snacks

**SERVES 4**

**A recipe from Errol McCosker.**

- *4 large pork sausages*
- *4 tbs. sweet mustard pickle*
- *2 cups mashed potato*
- *2 tbs. finely chopped chives or parsley (optional)*

Grill or fry sausages, cool slightly then split open lengthways. Spread with pickle. Mix chives through mashed potato and spoon onto sausages, place under grill and cook until golden brown.

*Optional: Sweet mustard pickle can be substituted with tomato sauce.*

# Sausages in Apples

**MAKES 4**

- *4 sausages*
- *4 large granny smith apples, cored*

Pierce sausages several times then press into centre of apples. Score the apple skin, place on a lined baking tray and bake in a 180°C oven for 1 hour.

# Vegetarian Mains

*Success usually comes to those who are too busy to be looking for it.*

Henry David Thoreau

---

## Asparagus & Egg Cakes

**MAKES 4**

- *6 free range eggs, hard boiled and chopped*
- *½ cup tinned asparagus cuts*
- *1 cup cooked mashed potato*
- *1 cup cooked rice*

Preheat oven to 180°C. Combine all ingredients and season with sea salt and pepper. Form into cakes, place on a lined baking tray and bake in oven for 20 minutes or until golden brown.

*Optional: Asparagus can be substituted with a 125g tin of corn kernels. Delicious served with a salad and dollop of aioli.*

*Tip: This is a great way to use any leftover rice.*

# Baked Rice Pilaf

**SERVES 4**

**A second generation recipe from the beautiful Fleur Welligan.**

- *1 onion, peeled and diced*
- *2 cloves garlic, chopped*
- *1 cup (185g) basmati rice*
- *2 cups (500ml) chicken stock*

Preheat oven to 180°C. Sauté onion in a little water. Add garlic and rice and stir. Add stock and bring to the boil. Transfer mixture to a baking dish, cover and bake for 30 minutes. Remove from oven and fluff rice with a fork.

*Optional: Stir through a knob of butter and some chopped parsley if desired.*

# Baked Ricotta Pie

**SERVES 4–6**

**This is super yummy served with a salad and delicious dressing!**

- *Olive oil spray*
- *1 kg fresh ricotta*
- *3 free range eggs, lightly beaten*
- *3 tbs. fresh thyme leaves*

Preheat oven to 200°C. Spray a 22cm round spring form cake tin with oil. Place ricotta and eggs in a bowl and stir to combine. Using a spatula, pour mixture into tin, sprinkle generously with thyme and season. Bake for 35–40 minutes or until firm and golden. Allow to cool before removing from tin.

*Optional: These can also be made in muffin trays, reduce baking time to 15 minutes or until the pies are firm and golden.*

# Bean Baskets

**MAKES 4**

- 4 flour tortillas
- 400g can Heinz Mean Beans Mexican, heated
- 125g coarsely grated cheese
- ¼ cup (80g) sour cream

Preheat oven 150°C. Mould tortillas into muffin pans and bake in oven for 5–6 minutes or until golden. Divide beans among baskets. Top with a dollop of sour cream and grated cheese.

# Buttered Couscous

**SERVES 4**

- 2½ cups (625ml) chicken stock
- 450g couscous
- 3 tbs. (45g) butter

Heat chicken stock in a saucepan, add couscous and butter. Mix well and allow to stand for 5 minutes before serving.

*Couscous Options:*
- *Roasted pumpkin dusted in Moroccan spice, finely diced red onion, toasted pinenuts*
- *Fresh parsley, mint, lemon juice and zest*
- *Tuna, finely diced red onion and coriander*
- *Toasted pine nuts, sultanas and fresh mint*
- *Red pepper, slivered almonds, sultanas and baby spinach*

# Cheddar & Basil Tortillas

**SERVES 1**

- *1 tbs. (15g) butter*
- *2 soft flour tortillas*
- *40g cheddar cheese, grated*
- *¼ cup fresh basil leaves*

Heat butter in a non-stick frying pan over medium heat. Add one tortilla, layer with cheese then basil and season with sea salt and pepper, cook for 2 minutes or until underneath is golden brown. Top with remaining tortilla and flip. Cook for a further 2–3 minutes. Slide from pan onto a chopping board and cut into wedges. Serve immediately with a salad.

*Optional: Substitute basil with semi-dried tomatoes, mushrooms, relish or whatever you like.*


# Cheesy Pasta Bake

**SERVES 4**

**A recipe by Marie McColl.**

- *45g pkt chicken and leek soup*
- *2½ cups (625ml) milk*
- *4 cups spiral shaped pasta, cooked (approx. 2 cups uncooked)*
- *75g tasty cheese, grated*

Preheat oven to 180°C. Combine soup and milk in a saucepan stirring until boiling. Combine with pasta and season with sea salt and pepper. Pour into a casserole dish and sprinkle with cheese. Bake in oven for 20 minutes.

# Curry Noodle Bowl

**SERVES 6**

- 3 x 85g instant noodles with vegetable flavouring
- 1 ltr. vegetable stock
- 1 tbs. red curry paste
- 500g pkt. mixed frozen stir fry vegies, thawed (or you can also use mixed fresh vegies)

Break noodles in a bowl. Combine seasoning packets, stock and curry paste in a large saucepan. Add 2½ cups (625ml) water and bring to boil, stirring regularly. Add noodles and vegetables. Cook for about 3 minutes, stirring occasionally until noodles are tender and vegetables are tender but crisp.


# Eggplant & Ricotta Pasta

**SERVES 4**

- 120g jar char-grilled, marinated eggplant
- 500g jar tomato and basil passata
- 450g penne pasta, cooked and drained
- 200g fresh ricotta

In a saucepan, add eggplant to passata and simmer for 10 minutes until warm. Divide pasta between four bowls and top with sauce and ricotta.

# Field Mushroom & Garlic Pizza

**MAKES 2**

**Recipe from Rodger Fishwick.**

- *2 pieces Turkish bread*
- *1–2 cloves garlic, crushed*
- *1 cup field mushrooms, sliced*
- *½ cup (125g) mozzarella cheese*

Preheat oven to 180°C. Place Turkish bread on a baking paper lined tray. Spread garlic over the bread and place the mushrooms on top. Sprinkle with mozzarella cheese and bake for 10 minutes.

# Frittata

**SERVES 4**

**A recipe by Katrina Price.**

- *6 free range eggs*
- *3 cups freshly chopped spinach*
- *150g parmesan cheese, grated*
- *½ cup (65g) breadcrumbs*

Preheat oven to 150°C. Beat the eggs with a whisk until light and fluffy, add spinach, cheese and breadcrumbs, season to taste. Line a baking tray with paper, pour in mixture and cook for 20 minutes.

# Maltese Cheese Pie

**SERVES 4–6**

**A recipe from Ralph Buttigieg.**

- *500g ricotta cheese*
- *¼ cup chopped parsley*
- *3 free range eggs*
- *2 sheets ready rolled puff pastry*

Preheat oven to 180°C. Combine the ricotta and parsley in a mixing bowl. Beat the eggs and add to mixture, reserving a small amount of egg to paint the top of the pie. Season with sea salt and pepper. Line a greased, or paper lined pie dish, with one sheet of pastry. Add the mixture and cover with remaining sheet, seal the edges with a fork and trim excess pastry. Cut 2–3 air holes in the lid and baste with remaining egg. Bake for 30–35 minutes or until pastry turns golden on top.

# Polenta & Zucchini (Courgette) Lasagne

**SERVES 6**

- 1 cup (170g) polenta
- 2–3 zucchinis (courgettes), grated
- 575g jar of creamy tomato pasta sauce
- 200g mozzarella, grated

Preheat oven to 180°C. Add 1 cup of polenta to 1 litre of boiling water, stir frequently until thick. Remove and allow to cool for 5 minutes. Roughly, divide polenta into a quarter and use the first quarter to thinly line the bottom of a rectangular baking dish. Cover the polenta with pasta sauce, zucchini and a third of the cheese, season. Continue for another 3 layers, ensuring last layer is mozzarella. Bake in oven for 30 minutes or until cheese is nice and brown on top. Enjoy with a yummy salad or roast vegies!

*Optional: Substitute zucchini for whatever vegetable you like eg.,mushrooms, sweet potato, baby spinach.*

# Potato Tortilla

**SERVES 4**

- ¼ cup (60ml) olive oil
- 2 peeled and sliced potatoes
- 8 free range eggs

Heat olive oil in a fry pan over medium heat. Cook potatoes for 2–3 minutes. Whisk eggs together and season. Pour over potatoes and cook for a further 10 minutes. Place under a hot grill for 2 minutes or long enough to brown. Allow to cool before cutting into wedges to serve.

*Hint: To keep eggs fresh, store in fridge in their carton as soon as possible after purchase. This is because an egg will age more in a day at room temperature than it will in a week in the fridge.*

# Spinach & Ricotta Quiche

**SERVES 4**

**A recipe by David Wilson.**

- *1 sheet ready rolled puff pastry*
- *2 large free range eggs*
- *250g ricotta cheese*
- *1½ cups shredded spinach*

Preheat oven to 180°C. Place pastry in a greased or paper lined quiche dish. Beat eggs, add ricotta and mix well. Add spinach and season with sea salt and pepper. Pour mixture into pastry and bake in oven for 25 minutes or until set.


# Spinach Pie

**SERVES 2**

**A recipe from Karyn Turnbull-Markus.**

- *2 cups shredded spinach*
- *250g cottage cheese*
- *2 free range eggs, whisked*
- *2 cloves garlic, crushed*

Preheat oven to 180°C. Boil spinach for 5 minutes, drain and then in a small oven proof dish, layer spinach, cottage cheese and garlic. After each layer, spoon over a little egg, continue until all ingredients are used, ensuring final layer is cottage cheese then season with cracked pepper. Bake in oven for 20 minutes or until pie is slightly brown on top.

# Sweet Potato & Feta Frittata

**SERVES 4**

- *1 large orange sweet potato, peeled and cubed*
- *2 tbs. (30ml) extra virgin olive oil*
- *200g feta, crumbled*
- *6 free range eggs*

Preheat oven to 200°C. Spread potato on a baking tray and sprinkle with half the oil. Bake for 20 minutes or until tender. Over medium heat, put remaining oil in a non-stick frying pan and add potato and feta. Whisk eggs and season with sea salt and pepper then pour over potato and feta. Reduce heat to low and cook for 5 minutes or until the base is set. Place frittata under medium preheated grill (ensure a heat proof handle) for 7 minutes or until cooked through. Allow to cool slightly then cut into wedges.

*Optional: This is delicious served with a fresh green salad.*

# Vegie Stack

**SERVES 2**

**Recipe by beautiful Boofy.**

- *1 tortilla*
- *500g sweet potato (or pumpkin) cut into 1 cm strips*
- *1 cup (200g) goats cheese or grated cheddar cheese*
- *2 large red peppers cut into 4 cm strips*

Preheat oven to 180°C. Boil sweet potato for 10 minutes. Sprinkle some water on peppers and lay on a baking paper lined tray, bake for 8 minutes or until cooked. Place tortilla in a round dish and layer with potato, peppers and cheese alternatively. Bake for about 35 minutes or until golden brown.

*Optional: Serve with sweet chilli sauce or sour cream or you can also sprinkle some finely chopped garlic to the layers too.*

# Desserts

*The best thing a Father can do for his children is to love their Mother!*

Unknown

## Apple Crumble

**SERVES 6**

**Simply scrumptious!**

- *2 x 400g can apples*
- *¼ cup (40g) sultanas*
- *220g pkt Hobnobs, crushed*
- *115g butter, melted*

Preheat oven to 180°C. Combine apple and sultanas, spoon into baking dish. Mix biscuits with butter and sprinkle over apple mixture. Bake for 15 minutes or until golden and serve with cream or custard.

**Another delicious variation from Lorraine Leeson.**

- *2 x 400g can apples*
- *115g butter, melted (extra for greasing)*
- *½ cup (110g) brown sugar*
- *200g pkt shortbread fingers, crushed*

Preheat oven to 180°C. Lightly grease a baking dish. Evenly layer apple across the base. Cream butter and sugar until mixture is quite fluffy. Mix in biscuits then spread evenly over apple. Bake for 30 minutes in oven until topping is golden.

*Optional: Cinnamon may be added to biscuit mixture if desired.*

# Baked Apples with a Twist

**MAKES 2**

**A recipe by Rob Watson. "D.e.l.i.c.i.o.u.s!"**

- *2 granny smith apples*
- *1 Mars bar, frozen and cut in half*
- *2 tbs. Muscat wine/ liqueur*
- *1 tsp. brown sugar*

Preheat oven to 180°C. Core the apples so half the Mars bar fits into the middle, wrap in foil like a bomb, gently fill each with 1 tbs. muscat and sprinkle with sugar. Bake in oven (or on top of bbq) for 20 minutes. The muscat will poach the apple and the Mars bar ooooozes everywhere.

*Optional: Serve with a scoop of ice cream.*

# Baked Ricotta with Blueberry Sauce

**SERVES 4–6**

**Kim's favourite, dish this up to the applause of all!**

- *2 free range egg whites*
- *6 tbs. honey*
- *250g cup ricotta cheese*
- *2 cups blueberries*

Preheat oven to 180°C. Beat egg whites until stiff peaks form. Mix through 4 tbs. honey and ricotta cheese. Once combined, pour into a small baking paper lined 18cm cake tin and bake for 40 minutes or until the pie rises and is golden. Meanwhile, place blueberries in a small frying pan and heat gently until softened. Stir through 2 tbs. honey and allow to simmer for 20 minutes. Serve blueberry sauce over ricotta pie wedges.

# Baked Rice Custard

**SERVES 4**

**This is really easy and really tasty!**

- *⅓ cup (60g) rice*
- *¾ cup (190ml) condensed milk*
- *3 free range eggs, lightly beaten*
- *¼ cup (40g) sultanas*

Preheat oven to 180°C. Cook rice in a large pan of boiling water for 10 minutes, drain. Combine condensed milk, eggs, rice and sultanas with 1¾ cups water and mix thoroughly. Pour into a shallow baking dish. Stand dish in baking pan with enough hot water to come halfway up sides of dish. Bake for 40 minutes or until set.

*Optional: Before baking sprinkle with nutmeg.*


# Bread & Butter Pudding

**SERVES 4**

**A yummy recipe from Ralph Buttigieg.**

- *2 tbs. butter*
- *4 slices thick raisin bread*
- *1½ cups (375ml) milk*
- *2 tbs. egg custard mix*

Preheat oven to 180°C. Butter the bread slices well and cut into fours. Layer bread into a greased oven proof dish. Mix the milk and custard powder until all the powder dissolves. Pour over bread and allow at least ½ hour for the bread to soak up the liquid. Bake for 15–20 minutes or until the top is golden brown. Allow to cool and enjoy!

*Optional: Spread bread with your favourite jam before baking.*

# Butterscoth Pumpkin Pie

**Serves 8 and is delightfully delicious!**

- *2 free range eggs*
- *375ml English toffee ice cream, melted*
- *1¼ cups mashed pumpkin*
- *1 pie crust or biscuit base*

Preheat oven to 180°C. Beat eggs until frothy. Add ice cream and pumpkin. Stir until smooth. Pour filling into pie crust and bake for about 45 minutes or until the filling is set. Cool and enjoy!

# Caramel & Coconut Ice cream

**SERVES 8**

- *600ml cream*
- *400g can Carnation caramel*
- *¼ cup (60ml) Bailey's liqueur*
- *¼ cup (30g) shredded coconut, toasted*

Combine cream, caramel and liqueur in large bowl and beat until thick and creamy with an electric mixer. Fold in coconut and pour into a paper lined baking tin, cover and freeze for at least 4-6 hours before serving.

# Caramel Pears

**SERVES 4**

- 2 large pears, peeled cored and cut into quarters
- ½ tbs. butter, melted
- 2 tbs. brown sugar
- 1½ tbs. cream

Preheat oven to 180°C. In a medium bowl, mix butter, sugar and cream. Into a baking dish place pear quarters and dollop with mixture. Bake for 8–12 minutes or until the mixture turns a light caramel colour and the pears are cooked through. Serve warm.


# Caramel Walnut Tarts

**MAKES 24**

**Recipe from Marie McColl.**

- 1½ sheets ready rolled shortcrust pastry, thawed
- 400g can Carnation caramel
- ½ cup (130g) smooth peanut butter
- 1½ cups (150g) chopped walnuts

Preheat oven to 200°C. Cut sheets into squares and press each square into non-stick mini-muffin trays. Bake for 8–10 minutes or until just golden, allow to cool. Whisk caramel and peanut butter until smooth, add 1 cup walnuts and stir through. Fill pastry cases with caramel mixture and sprinkle with remaining walnuts.

# Choc-Caramel Ravioli

**MAKES 16**

**Another from the talented Marie McColl.**

- *2 sheets ready rolled puff pastry*
- *2 Snickers bars, cut 2cm thick*

Preheat oven to 200°C. Line a baking tray with baking paper. Cut each sheet into approx. 16 squares, place 2 slices of Snickers onto the first 16 squares. Top with remaining squares, seal all 4 edges with a fork and trim excess pastry creating a neat ravioli effect. Bake 10–12 minutes or until puffed and golden.

*Optional: Delectable served with a creamy ice cream.*

# Chocolate Mousse Patty Cakes

**MAKES 6**

**Recipe from Wendy King.**

- *250g milk chocolate*
- *3 free range eggs*
- *¼ cup (45g) self raising flour*
- *250ml cream, whipped for serving*

Preheat oven to 180°C. Melt chocolate in a lightly heated saucepan stirring often to smooth. Mix eggs and flour with whisk and stir into chocolate. Place 6 patty cake papers into muffin tin and spoon in mixture. Bake for 20 minutes or until sides are set but centre is still liquid. Cool 10 minutes. Carefully remove paper, centres will be a warm mousse consistency. Top with a dollop of cream

*Optional: Sprinkle shaved chocolate on cream to make it look even MORE dazzling! Also delicious served with the following ice cream.*

# Cookies & Cream Ice cream

**A recipe from Jayne in Perth ... In her words "YUM – This is my hubby's fave!"**

- *400g can condensed milk*
- *600ml whipping cream*
- *200g high quality chocolate*
- *220g pkt plain chocolate biscuits*

Melt chocolate in a microwave, stirring every 30 seconds. Leave to stand and while cooling beat condensed milk and cream until thick, stir in melted chocolate and smashed bickies, pour into a paper lined tray, cover and freeze over night.

# Custard Tarts

**MAKES 12**

- *2 sheets ready rolled puff pastry, thawed*
- *500g premium vanilla custard*
- *3 tbs. brown sugar*

Preheat oven to 200°C. Cut 6 rounds from each sheet of pastry and line a non-stick muffin tray with them. Place a circle of baking paper with some uncooked rice on each and blind bake for 10-12 minutes. Remove paper and rice and allow to cool. Spoon an equal quantity of custard into each and sprinkle with brown sugar. Place tarts under a preheated grill allowing sugar to caramelise. Remove from heat and allow to cool slightly before serving.

*Optional: Another really lovely filling is Carnation caramel. Blind bake as above and cool before scooping in well beaten caramel. Top with a dollop of freshly whipped cream and fresh berries.*

# Frozen Yoghurt Tarts

**MAKES 20**

- *20 frozen mini tart shells, thawed*
- *1 cup (250g) thick strawberry yoghurt*
- *250g cream cheese, softened*
- *1 cup (320g) strawberry jam*

Preheat oven to 200°C. Place shells in oven 10 minutes or until golden brown and allow to cool. Beat remaining 3 ingredients until smooth. Spoon into tart shells and refrigerate for at least 2–3 hours before serving.

*Optional: Instead of frozen mini tart shells, use a pkt of round crunchy biscuits. Simply line a muffin tray with paper muffin shells and lay a biscuit in it. Distribute evenly with mixture.*


# Little Lemon Cheesecakes

**MAKES 8**

**Kim's hubby Glen's new f.a.v.o.u.r.i.t.e!**

- *250g cream cheese, softened*
- *280g jar lemon butter*
- *8 round, crunchy biscuits*

Line 8 holes of a muffin tray with paper muffin shells and place a buttersnap bickie flat side up in each. Using an electric mixer, beat cheese until creamy, then add all the lemon butter, mixing until nice and creamy. Spoon mixture onto biscuits and freeze for 2–3 hours or until firm. 5 minutes before serving, remove paper and serve decorated with fresh seasonal fruit.

# Lime Sherbert

**SERVES 6–8**

- 600ml whipping cream
- 400g can condensed milk
- 1 lime
- 3 free range egg whites

Combine cream, condensed milk, 2 tsp. lime rind and ¼ cup lime juice in large bowl and beat until thick with an electric beater. Beat egg whites until firm peaks form, fold into cream mixture. Pour into a freezer pan, cover and freeze for at least 4–6 hours before serving.

*Optional: If you don't have a freezer pan use a cake tin and line it with baking paper as it makes the ice cream easier to remove and serve. Lime can be successfully substituted with lemon.*


# Lisa's Upside Down Pear Tart

**SERVES 6**

**A recipe from the gorgeous Lisa Darr.**

- 2 tbs. (30g) butter (a little extra for glazing)
- ¼ cup (60g) real maple syrup
- 2 firm pears, peeled and sliced
- 2 sheets ready rolled puff pastry

Preheat oven to 180°C. In a frying pan, sauté butter and maple syrup until toffee like. Place pears in toffee and coat well. Cut a circle from ready rolled puff pastry (enough to cover bottom of pan) and glaze both sides with a little melted butter, lay over pears. Place frypan (ensure a heat proof handle) into oven and bake for 20 minutes or until pastry is crisp and golden. Invert onto a serving plate and enjoy!

*Optional: Serve with a dollop of cream or ice cream.*

# Matchsticks

**SERVES 4**

**These are Kim's childhood favourites that continue to stand the test of time!**

- *2 sheets ready rolled puff pastry, thawed*
- *250ml cream, whipped*
- *4 tbs. strawberry jam*
- *2 tbs. icing sugar*

Preheat oven to 200°C. Roll out pastry, thinning it slightly, cut into 4 lenghtways strips (may get 5). Line two baking trays with baking paper and place pastry on each. Prick well and chill for 15 minutes in freezer. Bake in oven for 8–10 minutes or until pale golden brown. Using an egg flip, carefully turn pastry and bake for a further 6–8 minutes. Remove from oven and allow to cool. Spread the first sheet with jam and the second with cream and join together so that plain pastry faces up. Top with a sprinkling of icing sugar.

# Peanut Butter Ice cream Pie

**SERVES 8–10**

**This IS S.E.N.S.A.T.I.O.N.A.L!**

- *1 ltr. creamy ice cream, softened*
- *1¼ cups (325g) crunchy peanut butter*
- *1 sweet biscuit base*

Beat ice cream and peanut butter in large bowl with an electric mixer until nice and smooth. Pour into the biscuit base and place in freezer for at least 3 hours prior to serving.

*Optional: Add 2 tbs. of cocoa or cinnamon to the biscuit base. Serve drizzled with the Hot Fudge Sauce (see Sauces) …*

# Pineapple Flummery

**SERVES 8 and is delicious!**

- 400g can crushed pineapple
- 1 pkt lemon flavoured jelly crystals
- 410ml can evaporated milk, chilled

Drain juice from tin of pineapple. Place juice and 1 tbs. cold water in a small saucepan over medium heat and bring to boil. Place jelly crystals in a bowl and add boiling pineapple juice mixture. Stir until jelly crystals dissolve. Refrigerate for 20 minutes or until mixture is almost set. With an electric mixer, beat chilled milk for 4–5 minutes or until the consistency of whipped cream, wash beaters. Beat jelly until frothy, then fold into thickened milk. Pour into serving bowl, cover with cling film and refrigerate for an hour or until firm.

*Optional: Serve with leftover pineapple mixed with a little chopped mint.*

# Plum Pudding

**SERVES 12**

**A recipe from Daphne Beutel ... This is a CHRISTMAS KNOCKOUT.**

- 2 cups (350g) self raising flour
- 1 cup (220g) sugar
- 1 kg pkt dried mixed fruit
- 1 tbs. bicarbonate of soda

Mix the first 3 ingredients together in a large bowl. Mix 2 cups of hot water with bi-carb. of soda, add to the mixture and mix with a knife. Cover and leave overnight. Mix well the next morning. Place in a damp floured cloth and tie very securely with kitchen string. Boil gently in a large saucepan for 3 hours ensuring it does not come off the boil, or boil dry. Remove cloth whilst pudding is still warm.

# Quick No-Fail Cheesecake

**SERVES 8**

**A recipe by the very clever Michelle Steffensen!**

- *A bought biscuit/tart base*
- *250g cream cheese, softened*
- *400g condensed milk*
- *Juice of 3 lemons*

Preheat oven to 180°C. Bake base in oven for 10 minutes or until golden brown. Mix remaining ingredients with an electric beater until smooth, then pour into the base. Allow to set in fridge overnight.

*Optional: Decorate with whipped cream, a passionfruit and the zest of a lemon!*

# Strawberry & Banana Skewers with Caramel Dip

**MAKES 12**

**Always sooooo popular!**

- *400g can Carnation caramel*
- *¼ cup (80ml) pouring cream*
- *500g strawberries, washed and hulled*
- *2 bananas, peeled and sliced*

Pour caramel and cream into a saucepan, bring to the boil and reduce heat simmering for 2 minutes. Pour mixture into jug, allow to cool. Thread strawberries and banana onto skewers and drizzle with caramel sauce when ready to serve.

*Hint: Always wash strawberries before you remove their stalks, otherwise water will get into the fruit and spoil their flavour.*

# Stuffed Apples

**MAKES 4**

**YUMMMMMMMMMMMMMMMY!!!**

- *4 large green apples*
- *1 cup leftover fruitcake or Christmas pudding*

Preheat oven to 180°C. Core apples, wrap in foil and bake in oven for 20 minutes. Remove foil and stuff with fruitcake, bake for a further 10 minutes. Serve warm with custard.

*Optional: Can sprinkle with cinnamon or substitute fruit cake for sultanas as Kim's Nana, Mary Moore, has been doing for decades.*


# Toblerone Mousse

**SERVES 6**

**Always a crowd pleaser!**

- *2 x 100g blocks dark Toblerone chocolate, broken*
- *4 free range eggs, separated*
- *300ml double cream*
- *2 tbs. Tia Maria (optional)*

Melt chocolate in microwave, stirring every 30 seconds. Cool slightly before adding egg yolks. Whip egg whites to a stiff peak. Whip cream until firm then fold into melted Toblerone. Add egg whites and liqueur, fold until mixed. Spoon mousse into serving dishes. Chill until set.

*Optional: Serve with cream or ice cream and fresh fruit.*

*Tip: Cream whips best chilled and in a cold metal mixing bowl.*

# Tropical Fruit Salad

**SERVES 4**

**Divine!**

- *1 ripe mango, diced*
- *8 lychees, peeled and quartered*
- *1 banana, peeled and sliced*
- *3 passionfruit*

Combine all and mix. Delicious served with ice cream or as an accompaniment to a sweet.


# Yoghurt Ice cream

**SERVES 8**

**A recipe from Joanne Mason.**

- *400g can condensed milk*
- *200g banana yoghurt (or flavour of your choosing)*
- *300ml double cream*

Mix well all ingredients in an empty ice cream container and pop into the freezer overnight. As an option, yoghurt can be replaced with banana, strawberries, mango or any fresh fruit you choose.

# Yummy Jaffa Parcels

**MAKES 8**

- 2 sheets frozen ready rolled puff pastry
- 125g dark chocolate, broken
- 1 orange

Preheat oven to 200°C. Cut each pastry sheet into 4 quarters. In a bowl, combine chocolate, zest (from entire orange) and diced orange. Place 2 tbs. of the mix in the centre of each sheet. Lift each corner to cover the mixture forming an envelope, seal well. Place on a paper lined baking tray and bake for 15 minutes or until golden.

*Optional: Serve dusted with icing sugar and a dollop of ice cream.*

# Drinks

*The only man who never makes a mistake, is the man who never does anything.*

Anonymous

---

## Affogato

**MAKES 1**

- *1 cup (250ml) of your favourite hot, espresso coffee*
- *1 scoop of vanilla ice cream*

This looks fabulous served in a glass. Dollop ice cream into coffee. Serve immediately.

*Optional: For an extra indulgence pour a little Baileys over the ice cream.*

## Banana and Strawberry Smoothie

**MAKES 1**

**Recipe by dynamic Nutritionist Cyndi O'Meara.**

- *1 cup (250ml) milk or natural yoghurt*
- *1 banana*
- *6 strawberries*
- *1 tbs. honey*

Put all ingredients into a blender and mix until smooth.

# Berry Smoothie

**MAKES 2**

- *1 cup fresh berries*
- *2 cups (500ml) chilled milk*
- *4 scoops vanilla ice cream*

Place all ingredients in a blender with 6 blocks of ice and blend until smooth. Pour into tall glasses and serve.


# Blueberry Smoothie

**MAKES 1**

- *1 cup blueberries*
- *1 cup (250ml) chilled milk*
- *2 scoops strawberry ice cream*

Pop all ingredients in a blender and blend until smooth. Pour into tall glass and serve.


# Green Fizz

**MAKES 2**

- *¼ honeydew melon, chopped*
- *1 kiwi fruit*
- *2 cups (500ml) lemon and lime mineral water*

Blend melon and kiwi fruit. Add mineral water and garnish with ice cubes and a slice of lime.

# Green Grape Smoothie

**MAKES 2**

- *Slice of lime*
- *2 cups green seedless grapes*
- *1 cup diced pineapple*

Place ingredients in a blender with 1 cup (250 ml) cold water and 1 cup ice cubes, blend until smooth. Pour into glasses and serve.

# Fruity Christmas Punch

**A recipe from Jennette McCosker served up to rave reviews each Xmas!**

- *2 punnets of strawberries, reserve a few*
- *1.5 ltr. orange juice*
- *2 ltr. lemonade*

Puree strawberries and place in a bowl. Stir in orange juice and with reserved strawberries, slice and add. Mix in lemonade and serve over ice in tall glasses … *Cheers Santa!*

# Lemonade

**SERVES 4–6**

- *¾ cup (185ml) lemon juice, freshly squeezed*
- *¼ cup (60g) sugar*
- *1.25 ltr. soda water*

Place juice and sugar in saucepan over low heat, stir until sugar has dissolved. Simmer for 3 minutes to create syrup and cool in fridge. Pour cold lemon syrup into a large jug over ice-cubes, top with soda water. Stir before serving.

# Lychee Pineapple Cocktail

**MAKES 1**

**A recipe from Julie Forato who says: "This recipe is a real winner – great for breakfast, brunch, lunch, or as a pre-dinner cocktail with a shot of vodka!"**

- *5 lychees with half a cup of syrup (from tin)*
- *15 mint leaves*
- *½ cup (125ml) pineapple juice*
- *10 ice cubes*

Place all ingredients into a blender, and blend together until the ice is completely crushed. Serve in a glass garnished with mint leaves.


# Mango Smoothie

**MAKES 2**

- *4 frozen mango cheeks*
- *2 cups (500ml) cold milk*
- *1 tsp. ground cardamom*

Blend mango and milk until smooth. Pour into glasses, sprinkle with cardamom and serve.

# Marshmallow Hot Chocholate

**MAKES 1**

- 1 tbs. drinking chocolate
- 1 cup (250ml) milk
- 3 marshmallows

For each serve, blend drinking chocolate and milk in a saucepan. Add marshmallows and stir over heat until mixture almost boils. Pour into mug and enjoy!

# Mint Tea

**MAKES 2**

- 8–10 fresh mint leaves
- 2 slices lemon
- ½ tsp. Sugar

Boil 2 cups (500ml) of water and pour into a teapot. Add mint leaves and allow to infuse for 5 minutes. Serve with a slice of lemon and sugar to taste.

*Hint: A few finely chopped mint leaves will add a fresh flavour and fragrance to practically any cool soft drink.*

# Pineapple Banana Smoothie

**SERVES 2**

- 1 cup (250ml) orange juice
- 1 cup (250ml) pineapple juice
- 2 frozen bananas
- 2 dates, pitted

Blend all ingredients with 6 cubes of ice until smooth, then serve.

# Pineapple Tea Punch

**SERVES 2**

- *1 ripe pineapple*
- *12 mint leaves*
- *2 cups (500ml) cold black tea*
- *2 cups (500ml) dry ginger ale*

Peel pineapple and remove core, chop roughly. Place half of the pineapple with half the black tea and mint leaves into a blender for 30 seconds. Add the remaining pineapple and black tea and blend for another 30 seconds. Refrigerate and just before serving stir in ginger ale.


# Slime Shots

**MAKES 4**

- *1 pkt of aeroplane jelly crystals*
- *4 scoops of chocolate ice cream*
- *3 tbs. milk*

Prepare jelly according to the packet instructions and leave to set for 30 minutes. Place the ice cream and milk in a bowl and mash roughly with a fork until the ice cream is soft. Layer small spoonfuls of ice cream and jelly into 4 small glasses.


# Watermelon Refresher

- *1 kg seedless watermelon, coarsely chopped*
- *¾ cup (185ml) chilled orange juice, freshly squeezed*
- *3 tbs. lime juice, freshly squeezed*

Blend with ice. Garnish with a slice of lime.

*Optional: Grate in a tsp. of orange and lime zest.*

# If a Child Lives with Criticism

If children live with criticism, *they learn to condemn*

If children live with hostility, *they learn to fight*

If children live with fear, *they learn to be apprehensive*

If children live with pity, *they learn to feel sorry for themselves*

If children live with ridicule, *they learn to be shy*

If children live with jealousy, *they learn what envy is*

If children live with shame, *they learn to feel guilty*


If children live with tolerance, *they learn to be patient*

If children live with encouragement, *they learn to be confident*

If children live with praise, *they learn to appreciate*

If children live with approval, *they learn to like themselves*

If children live with acceptance, *they learn to find love in the world*

If children live with recognition, *they learn to have a goal*

If children live with sharing, *they learn to be generous*

If children live with honesty and fairness,
*they learn what truth and justice are*

If children live with security,
*they learn to have faith in themselves and in those around them*

If children live with friendliness,
*they learn that the world is a nice place in which to live*

If children live with serenity, *they learn to have peace of mind.*

## With what are your children living with?

**Dorothy L. Nolte**

# For The Children

*Children will soon forget your presents,
they will always remember your presence*

Dobson

---

# Savoury

## Asparagus Rolls

**MAKES 8**

- *8 slices wholemeal bread*
- *1 tbs. (15g) butter*
- *8 asparagus spears*

Remove crusts from bread and roll thin with a rolling pin. Lightly butter before placing an asparagus spear diagonally on each slice, roll tightly and cut in half.

*Optional: These are nice baked as well.*

# Basic Pizza Dough

- *1 sachet dried yeast*
- *½ tsp. salt*
- *2½ cups (430g) plain flour*
- *2 tbs. extra virgin olive oil*

Combine yeast and 1 cup warm water, cover and leave for 20 minutes. In a separate bowl, sift flour, add salt and make a well. Add the yeast mixture and oil. Mix with flat blade knife, using a cutting action, until a dough forms. Knead for 10 minutes or until smooth. Place in an oiled bowl, cover with cling film and leave for 45 minutes or until doubled in size.

# Chihuahuas

**MAKES 6**

**A favourite recipe by residents at Torbay Aged Care & Retirement Village Hervey Bay, Queensland, Australia.**

- *6 mini bread rolls*
- *6 chipolatas*
- *1 tbs. butter*
- *4 tsp. tomato sauce*

Grill chipolatas for about 10 minutes or until cooked. Slice the rolls vertically and spread with butter. Insert sausage and drizzle with tomato sauce and serve warm.

# Chicken Carnival Cones

**MAKES 8**

**A recipe by Isobele Whiting and enjoyed by EVERYONE!**

- *8 flour tortillas*
- *2 cups leftover roast chicken, shredded*
- *1 cup (175g) salsa*
- *125g cheddar cheese, grated*

Preheat oven to 180°C. Fold tortilla in half (if small, fold only the bottom third up) and roll into a cone. Fill bottom of cone with chicken, dollop 2 tsp. salsa before covering with a layer of cheese. Place on a paper lined baking tray and repeat the process until all ingredients are used. Bake in oven for 15 minutes.

# Chicken, Mango & Chickpea Burgers

**MAKES 12**

- *400g chickpeas, drained*
- *500g lean chicken mince*
- *4–5 tbs. mango chutney*
- *2 salad onion tops, finely chopped*

Process chickpeas, combine with remaining ingredients and season. Shape into burger cakes and cook in a non-stick frying pan over a moderate heat for 3 minutes. Flip and cook for another 3 minutes or until cooked through. Serve on a fresh roll with a slice of tomato and lettuce.

# Chicken Nuggets

**SERVES 4**

**They'll loooove them!**

- *2 chicken breasts, cut into nugget size pieces*
- *1 cup (260g) whole-egg mayonnaise*
- *1 cup (120g) seasoned stuffing mix*

Preheat oven to 180°C. Coat chicken with mayonnaise and then roll in stuffing mix. Place on a paper lined baking tray and into the oven for 20 minutes.


# Easy Peasy Fish Cakes

**MAKES 6**

**A recipe from the lovely Robyn Mayeke.**

- *1 cup cooked, flaked fish*
- *1 cup mashed potato*
- *½ cup fresh peas*
- *1 free range egg*

Simply mix altogether, roll into balls and lightly pan fry. Serve with salad.

# Easy Potato Bake

**SERVES 2—4 depending on how hungry your children are!**

- *2 potatoes*
- *½ cup (125ml) pouring cream*
- *½ cup (125ml) milk*
- *1 tbs. nutmeg*

Finely slice potatoes and layer in a greased pie dish. Mix cream and milk together and pour over potatoes. Sprinkle with nutmeg and bake in moderate oven for 30 minutes or until potatoes are cooked and golden brown.


# Frankfurt Pasta Bake

**SERVES 4**

- *2 frankfurters, sliced*
- *4 cups cooked penne pasta (approx. 2 cups uncooked)*
- *500g jar of favourite pasta sauce*
- *1 cup grated cheddar cheese*

Preheat oven to 180°C. Mix frankfurters, pasta and sauce together, use ¾ of the jar of sauce and add more if needed. Spoon the mixture into a baking dish and sprinkle with cheese. Bake for 20 minutes.

*Hint: Freeze remaining sauce for use at a later date.*

# Gourmet Sausages

**SERVES 6**

**A beauty from Marie McColl.**

- *6 of your favourite flavoured sausages*
- *2 sheets ready rolled puff pastry, thawed*

Preheat oven to 180°C. Cut pastry into thirds, place a sausage at the edge of each and roll. Press the edge lightly with a fork to seal and cut excess pastry from lengths if necessary. Bake for 20–25 minutes or until pastry is golden. Slice into small bites and serve with favourite dipping sauce.

*Optional: These are great served up as finger food at a bbq as well!*


# Hummus Sausage

**SERVES 2**

**Soooo quick and easy, recipe by the very suave Tony Van Dijk.**

- *4 herbed or Italian flavoured sausages*
- *4 tsp. hummus*
- *1 lemon, quartered*

Grill or sauté the sausages and serve with a dollop of hummus and a lemon wedge.

# Mini Cheese Quiches

**MAKES 6**

**A recipe from the gorgeous Michelle Fredericks.**

- *6 slices of bread, crusts removed*
- *100g cheddar cheese, grated*
- *1 tbs. mixed herbs*
- *2 large free range eggs, lightly beaten*

Preheat oven to 200°C. Press bread into non-stick muffin cups. Fill each cup with cheese and herbs and a sprinkle of pepper. Top each evenly with egg mixture and bake for 15 minutes or until set.


# Mouse Traps

**SERVES 1**

**Recipe by Wendy King.**

- *2 slices day old bread*
- *1 slice rindless bacon, cut in half*
- *2 slices tasty cheese*

Remove the sides of the bread. Lay a slice of cheese on each piece and top with a slice of bacon. Place under grill and cook until bacon is crispy. Cut lengthways into 3 fingers and serve.

# Peanut Butter Toasties

**SERVES 2**

- *2 slices wholemeal bread*
- *2 tbs. peanut butter*
- *2 tbs. sultanas*
- *⅓ cup grated cheddar cheese*

Grill one side of the bread slices until golden. Turn and spread with peanut butter then sprinkle with sultanas and top with cheese. Grill until cheese is melted, cut in half to serve.


# Pine Tomato Chicken

**SERVES 4**

- *400g can crushed or diced tomatoes*
- *5 tbs. pineapple juice (use 90% plus juice)*
- *3 tbs. vinegar*
- *8 skinless chicken drumsticks*

Preheat oven to 200°C. Mix diced tomato, pineapple and vinegar together to make a marinade. Place chicken in a casserole dish and pour marinade over the top of each piece. Cover and refrigerate for 2 hours, cover and cook chicken for around 40-50 minutes or until cooked throughout.

*Optional: Serve with rice and freshly steamed vegetables.*

# Savoury Fritters

**MAKES 10**

**Children love these.**

- 1 pkt 2 minute chicken noodles
- 4 free range eggs, lightly beaten
- 2 salad onion tops, finely chopped
- 2 rashers rindless bacon, chopped and lightly fried

Cook noodles (without flavouring) then drain. Combine noodles with flavour sachet, eggs, salad onion tops and bacon. Place egg rings in a non-stick frying pan and spoon enough mixture to fill the ring, cook on both sides until golden.

# Tacos

**MAKES 2**

- 2 taco shells
- 260g lean beef mince
- ⅓ cup (60g) pasta sauce
- 1 cup shredded lettuce

Cook mince in a non-stick frying pan until brown and add pasta sauce. Simmer on low heat for 5 minutes. Alternate a thin layer of mince with a thin layer of lettuce till each taco is full.

*Optional: You can also add sliced mushrooms, peas and shredded carrot to the mince mix too.*

# Tasty Fish

**SERVES 5**

- *10 fish fingers*
- *300g can condensed tomato soup*

Preheat oven to 180°C. Place fingers in a baking dish. Cover with soup and bake for 45 minutes. Serve with chips and vegies.


# Yummy Bean Grill

**MAKES 2**

- *150g can baked beans*
- *1–2 tbs. finely chopped parsley*
- *2 slices wholemeal bread, lightly toasted*
- *2 thin slices mozzarella cheese*

Combine beans and parsley and spread over toast. Top with mozzarella and place under preheated grill until cheese melts.

# Sweet

*When buying chocolate, bear in mind that the higher the percentage of cocoa solids, the higher the quality of chocolate, and the less sugar it has.*

The best quality has 70% cocoa solids.

---

## Basic Biscuits

**MAKES ABOUT 70**

**"Very good value for money!"**

- *1 cup (220g) sugar*
- *500g butter*
- *5 cups (875g) self raising flour*
- *400g can condensed milk*

Preheat oven to 180°C. Cream sugar and butter until white and fluffy. Sift in flour, and pour in condensed milk. Mix to combine. Roll into teaspoon size balls and place on paper lined baking tray. Flatten slightly with a fork. Bake in oven for 10–12 minutes or until golden.

*Optional: Anything can be added to the basic mix to give variety, such as; smarties, cornflakes, sultanas, finely diced apple, cinnamon, choc chips etc. For a healthier version, use half wholemeal flour.*

*NB: Mixture will freeze. Roll into balls, and place in container layering with non-stick paper. Thaw slightly before cooking.*

# Bran Bars

**MAKES 8**

- 6 cups (720g) Sultana Bran
- ½ cup (80g) dried apricots, chopped
- 4 tbs (60g) butter
- 1 cup marshmallows

Combine cereal and apricots in a bowl. Melt butter in a saucepan over medium heat, add marshmallows, stirring until smooth. Pour in cereal and stir until coated. Press into a paper lined baking tin (approx 20 x 30 cm) and chill until firm. Slice ready for the lunch boxes.

*Optional: Any dried fruit can be used, is delicious with dried mango too! Alternatively they are nice set in patty papers.*


# Caramels

**MAKES 16**

- 115g soft butter (plus a little extra for greasing)
- 4 tbs. brown sugar
- 2 tbs. golden syrup
- ½ can condensed milk

Boil ingredients for 15 minutes, stirring frequently to prevent burning. Pour into a paper lined tin and when nearly set, mark in squares. Cut when chilled.

# Caramel Biscuits

**MAKES 20**

**A recipe enjoyed by Riley Warrener and Liam Cooperthwaite.**

- *115g softened butter*
- *½ cup (110g) brown sugar*
- *2 tbs. golden syrup*
- *1 cup (175g) self raising flour*

Preheat oven to 180°C. Cream butter and sugar with an electric mixer. Add syrup and beat until fluffy. Mix in flour until texture is such that you are able to roll into balls. Place on a paper lined baking tray and allow for spreading, press each gently with a fork and bake in oven for 15 minutes.


# Caramel Choc Truffles

**MAKES 30**

**A recipe from Marie McColl ... They will be devoured!**

- *400g can Carnation caramel*
- *2 tbs. butter*
- *250g plain chocolate biscuits, crushed*
- *¾ cup (90g) desiccated coconut*

Combine caramel and butter in a pan, bring to boil stirring, remove from heat. Add biscuit crumbs and mix well. Refrigerate for 1 hour. Roll heaped teaspoons of mixture into balls, coat in coconut, chill until firm.

*Optional: Make a double batch as they freeze well.*

# Caramello Pears

**MAKES 6**

**Recipe by Kylie Burborough NZ ... Loved by 6 year olds and 60 year olds!**

- *3 ripe pears*
- *1 pkt caramel Rollos*

Preheat oven to 180°C. Cut the pears in half and core out seeds to make a shallow gully in the flesh. Top with 2–3 caramel Rollos and bake until the chocolate has melted.


# Chocolate Scrunch

**MAKES 18**

**A recipe from Michelle Dodd. Scrunch has a yummy crunchy texture and is super easy to make — kids love it and it goes well with coffee too!**

- *200g dark chocolate*
- *1 cup (80g) rice bubbles*
- *½ cup (60g) desiccated coconut*
- *¼ cup (40g) dried apricots, finely chopped, or other dried fruit*

Put the chocolate into a heatproof bowl, place over a pan of simmering water and stir frequently until the chocolate has melted. Fold in the rice bubbles, coconut and dried fruit and mix well.
Tip onto a paper lined baking tray and spread to a thin, even layer. Neaten edges then refrigerate till set. Cut into squares and enjoy!

# Date Slice

**A great sweet treat!**

- 1 cup (240g) chopped dates
- 125g butter
- ½ cup (100g) caster sugar
- 2 cups (160g) rice bubbles

Bring 1½ cups of water to boil, add dates and boil for 5 minutes. Remove from heat and drain. Cream butter and sugar with an electric beater until smooth then add dates and rice bubbles. While warm press into a paper lined baking tin. Cut into squares and set in fridge.

# Fruit Dip

**MAKES 1 CUP**

- 1 cup (250g) natural Greek yoghurt
- ½ tsp. ground cinnamon
- 3 tbs. fruit jam

Place all ingredients into a bowl and mix well. Chill for at least 2 hours prior to serving to allow flavours time to develop. Serve with a platter of fresh fruit for dipping.

# Fruit Medley

**SERVES 8**

- 4 nectarines, chopped
- 2 bananas, sliced
- 1 cup blueberries
- 1 tbs. orange juice

Combine all ingredients in a bowl and gently toss. Cool in fridge before serving.


# Hit The Road Bars

**MAKES 12**

- 4 cups (400g) small rolled oats
- 2 cups (320g) natural almonds, coarsely chopped
- ¾ can condensed milk
- 115g butter, melted

Preheat oven to160°C. Combine all ingredients in a large bowl and mix well. Spread in a well greased baking tin and bake in oven for 25 minutes or until golden. Allow to stand until slightly cooled then cut while still warm.

# Jaxson's Double Choc Strawberries

**This is fantastic for little kids and big kids!!!**

- *A big punnet of strawberries, washed*
- *100g dark chocolate*
- *65g white chocolate*

Place strawberries in the fridge to chill. Melt dark and white chocolate separately. Dip strawberries in the dark chocolate ¾ the way up to the top of the chocolate, return to the fridge to set. Dip the chilled choc dipped strawberries into the white chocolate about 1 cm up so it's just covering the strawberry tips. Serve chilled.


# Jam Drops

**MAKES 60**

**Recipe by Joy Duke.**

- *250g butter, softened*
- *1 cup (200g) caster sugar*
- *2 cups (350g) plain flour*
- *Jam of choice*

Preheat oven to 175°C. Cream butter and sugar with an electric beater until light and fluffy. Fold in flour and spoon into heaped dollops onto a paper lined baking tray. Use the end of a wooden spoon to push a hole nearly to the base of the biscuit dough. Fill hole with jam of choice and bake for 15 minutes or until slightly golden. Remove from oven and allow to cool before serving.

*Optional: Dust with icing sugar to jazz them up a bit for adult afternoon teas.*

# Jelly in Oranges

**MAKES 6**

**This is a sparkling dessert at children's parties!**

- *3 ripe oranges*
- *1 pkt raspberry jelly, set*

Cut oranges in half, remove flesh and fill with jelly.

*Optional: Top with a little ice cream and sprinkle with 100's and 1,000's.*


# Mallow Pears

**MAKES 4**

**A recipe by our lovely Aunty Nikki Ogawa.**

- *2 pears, halved and deseeded*
- *8 marshmallows*
- *¼ tsp. nutmeg*

Place pear halves on a microwave safe dish and cover with glad wrap. Microwave for 1 minute. Remove and top each pear with 2 marshmallows and a sprinkle of nutmeg. Grill under moderate heat until marshmallows are golden brown. Serve warm.

# Melon Ice Blocks

**MAKES 5 CUPS**

- *4 cups chopped, seedless watermelon*
- *2 cups chopped fresh pineapple*

Combine all ingredients and blend, in batches, until smooth. Pour into iceblock moulds and freeze.

*Optional: Watermelon can be substituted with 2 cups of honeydew melon.*


# Peppermint Chocolate Slice

**This is BRILLIANT and so very easy the kids can do it!**

- *375g dark chocolate melts*
- *3 drops peppermint essence*
- *190g white chocolate melts*
- *4 drops green food colouring*

Line 20cm square cake tin with baking paper or foil. Melt dark chocolate melts in a lightly heated saucepan, stirring throughout melting process. Add peppermint essence and stir. Spread half the mixture evenly over bottom of tin. Set in fridge for 5 minutes.

Melt white chocolate melts the same way then stir in green food colouring. Spread this over layer of dark chocolate and then refrigerate until set. Spread remaining dark chocolate over white/green chocolate and set in fridge Cut into pieces and store in fridge.

*Hint: To make fun ice cubes for a party, add a drop or two of food colouring to the ice cube tray, you can make different colours for a pretty rainbow effect.*

# Raisin Dainties

**MAKES 12**

- 2 cups (240g) cornflakes, crushed
- ½ cup (60g) desiccated coconut
- 1 cup (170g) raisins
- 400g can condensed milk

Preheat oven to 160°C. Mix all ingredients well. Line a fairy cake tin with papers and evenly distribute mixture. Bake in oven for 15 minutes or until nicely browned.


# Trail Mix

**Recipe from Lea Van Dijk.**

- 4 cups (500g) mixed nuts
- 1 cup (170g) raisins or sultanas
- 1 cup (160g) of dried apricots, chopped
- 250g dark chocolate, chopped into various sized pieces

Mix all together and store in cool area. Can also place into zip lock bags ready to grab and go.

# Vanilla Ice cream

**MAKE 2 LITRES**

**A terrific little recipe by the gorgeous Carly Nelson.**

- *1 ltr. pouring cream*
- *1 ltr. full cream milk*
- *2 tbs. vanilla*
- *¾ cup (160g) brown sugar*

Mix all ingredients together until thoroughly combined. Place in freezer for at least 4 hours prior to serving. Easy and cheap!

*Optional: Mix in some flaked chocolate or fresh fruit for variety – everyone will love it!*


# Yogo Tropo

**SERVES 1**

**Recipe by the beautiful Maddie Willson created for a school assignment.**

- *1 Kiwi fruit, peeled and diced*
- *6 strawberries, washed, hulled and halved*
- *½ a banana, sliced*
- *200g tub vanilla yoghurt*

Into a glass place a layer of strawberries, top with a dollop of yoghurt, then a layer of kiwi fruit, a dollop of yoghurt, a layer of banana, strawberries and kiwi fruit and a final dollop of yoghurt. Decorate with leftover fruit and serve

*Optional: Maddie says "Make this with any seasonal fruits!"*

# Think Inside The Box

*An investment in knowledge always pays the best interest.*

Benjamin Franklin

---

We all know it is imperative children get the right nutrients during the day to help sustain high levels of concentration and energy ... Yet often we struggle to make lunch boxes fun, healthy and eaten! Given that lunch provides around *one quarter* of a child's daily nutritional requirements, it's in their best interests to fuel their bodies with great growing food and in our best interests to know they actually eat what is given to them. Remember, where possible try to balance meals and lunch boxes so that children have something from each food group.

The food groups are:

1. *Bread, cereals, rice, pasta, noodles*
2. *Vegetables and legumes*
3. *Fruit*
4. *Milk, yoghurt, cheese and fish*
5. *Meat, poultry, eggs, nuts and legumes*

*For example; a wholemeal sandwich with chicken, cucumber and cheese, a quartered orange, carrot sticks and yoghurt covers all the bases.*

To keep children interested, change what you place in their lunchboxes each day. As well as providing carbohydrate, protein and healthy fat, this will ensure a diverse range of nutrients to keep those beautiful little bodies in peak condition inside and out.

# Sensible Lunchbox Tips

Here are some tips gathered from many a wise Mum at our children's schools and kindergartens that may just help.

- *Buy a lunchbox that is airtight so you don't have to wrap food in plastics and foils*

- *Such lunchboxes also allow you to make sandwiches the night before and store in the fridge. They will stay as fresh as if they were in wrapping.*

- *If your school or kindy doesn't have a fridge, place lunchboxes and drink bottles into an insulated lunch bag to keep cool.*

- *Alternatively use a frozen brick.*

- *Try to chill cooked foods such as egg, bolognaise etc. before packing (the zone for bugs to start is 50°C – 60°C so ensure all food is kept well below this temperature range).*

- *Encourage children to swish their water around their mouths after eating to briefly wash their teeth.*

- *Add a piece of sliced cheese to lunches, especially when you have included something a little naughty as cheese will help to protect teeth from decay.*

- *Don't give your child nuts or foods that need supervision if you are unsure whether they are being watched over while they eat.*

- *Peel a pear or apple and soak in water that has the juice of ½ a lemon for a few minutes, it won't turn brown.*

# Lunchbox Sushi

**SERVES 2**

**Presents beautifully and are very popular in our households!**

- *4 slices soya and linseed bread*
- *1 tbs. whole egg mayonnaise*
- *½ avocado, mashed*
- *½ cucumber*

Remove crusts and, with a rolling pin, gently roll bread to flatten slightly. Along the middle of each slice spread a little mayonnaise and avocado. Place long, thin strips of cucumber on top and roll tightly. Cut in thirds, turn up and place into lunchbox for later.

*Optional: Use a variety of breads.*

Other yummy fillings:

- *Cream cheese, salmon and thin slices of cucumber*
- *Vegemite or Marmite and thin slices of cheese*
- *Ham, cheese and finely shredded lettuce*
- *Cottage cheese, thinly sliced carrot and sultanas*
- *Peanut butter and thinly sliced carrot*
- *Egg and lettuce*
- *Grated apple, sultanas and cream cheese*
- *Tuna, mayonnaise and finely shredded lettuce*
- *Curried egg*
- *Avocado, shredded chicken and cheese*

For a sweeter variety do the same as above but use fruit or raisin loaf slices and fill with the following:

- *Strawberry jam and cream cheese*
- *Peanut butter and honey*
- *Mashed banana*
- *Peanut butter and mashed banana*
- *Nutella and grated apple*
- *Pineapple*
- *Peanut butter and strawberry jam*
- *Cottage cheese, jam and sultanas*

# Skyscraper Sandwiches

**SERVES 2**

**Morgan McCosker looooves these in his lunchbox!**

- *6 slices bread*
- *2 slices cheese*
- *2 slices ham*
- *½ cup shredded lettuce*

Remove crusts and on two pieces of bread place a slice of cheese and ham. Cover with another piece of bread, add lettuce and top with final slice of bread. Cut each in half and stack one on top of another to form two skyscraper sandwiches!

*Optional: Vary the fillings to whatever your children will eat.*

# For The Baby & Toddlers

*Wherever possible – breastfeeding is the best source of nutrition for your child, so it's best to feed for as long as you can. When your child is ready to transfer to solids, introduce lumpy foods after three to five weeks of pureed food. Gradually make it lumpier because this will help baby learn to chew even if he has no teeth. Add finger foods thereafter. By the time baby reaches his first birthday he should be eating regular family food with some modifications.*

---

## Avocado Dip with Goats Cheese

**Recipe by our very clever chiropractor Dr Sarah Farrant.**

- ½ avocado
- 1 tbs. goats cheese
- 1 tbs. tomato sauce
- A squeeze of lemon juice

Blend all ingredients until thin in consistency. Serve to baby on a teaspoon.

## Avocado Yoghurt

- ¼ avocado, mashed well
- 1 tbs. yoghurt

Mix both well and serve immediately.

*Optional: Replace yoghurt with orange juice and add 1 tsp. rice cereal mix well and serve immediately.*

# Baby Meatballs

**Recipe by Janelle McCosker.**

- *250g lean mince*
- *½ cup mashed potatoes*

Preheat oven to 180°C. Combine ingredients and mix well. Roll into little balls and place on baking tray and cook for around 20 minutes. Drain of excess liquid then cool and serve.

*Optional: Grate in some zucchini (courgette) or a little cheese.*


# Banavo

**Recipe by Kim Morrison ... They are sure to looooove this one!**

- *¼ avocado*
- *¼ banana*
- *½ tsp. manuka honey*

Mash well together and serve.


# Fruit Gel

- *1 sachet gelatine*
- *½ cup (125ml) fruit juice*

Dissolve gelatine in ½ cup boiling water, add fruit juice and mix well. Pour mixture into a bowl and cover, cool and store in refrigerator to set.

# Fruity Teething Treat

**Rachael made these throughout the time Jaxson teethed and it was heaven on a stick for him!**

- *1 punnet strawberries, hulled*
- *2 cups diced watermelon*
- *2 apples, cored and sliced*
- *½ mango*

Blend all ingredients well and freeze into ice cube trays with a mini ice lolly stick inserted into each when half frozen. The children can hold onto them and suck away on the frozen fruit, it's nutritious and soothing all at the same time!


# Lamb & Barley Cassoulet

- *100g diced lamb*
- *2 tbs. barley*
- *½ carrot*
- *Pinch dried sage*

Pre-heat oven to 180°C. Place all ingredients in a casserole dish with 1 cup boiling water. Place on the stovetop and bring to the boil. Remove, cover and place in oven for 45 minutes. Blend for smaller babies. Perfect for freezing in ice cube trays.

*Optional: Add a little tomato paste or diced tomato for extra flavour.*

# Orange Delight

**MAKES 2**

**Recipe by Cyndi O'Meara – perfect for an after school summer snack!**

* *2 oranges*

Insert an ice lolly stick into a peeled orange and freeze for an hour or two.

# Prune Juice

* *12 prunes*

Soak prunes in water for 2 hours. Strain liquid into a saucepan. Bring to boil and add prunes. Reduce heat and simmer for 10 minutes or until tender. Strain juice and store in a sealed container in the fridge.

# Pumpkin Soup

**Pumpkin – a yummy baby food, loaded with Vitamin A and other nutrients.**

* *250g pumpkin, peeled and chopped*
* *¼ tsp. nutmeg*
* *½ cup cooked rice*

Place all ingredients in a saucepan with 2 cups of water, cover and bring to boil. Reduce heat and simmer for 15 minutes or until tender. Blend until smooth.

*Optional: Use 2 cups of homemade stock if desired and substitute pumpkin for any vegetable.*

# Quick & Easy Cheese Sauce

**MAKES 1 CUP**

- *8 tbs. cream cheese, softened*
- *25g parmesan cheese, grated*
- *⅓ cup (80ml) milk*
- *Pinch nutmeg*

Place the cream cheese, parmesan and milk in a suitable dish and microwave on medium for 6–8 minutes, stirring every 2 minutes. When the sauce is smooth, stir in the nutmeg. Toss the sauce with hot, cooked pasta.

# Savoury Vegetables

**A recipe from Lisa Darr.**

- *1 cup mashed potato and pumpkin*
- *¼ tsp. vegemite or marmite*
- *2 tbs. grated cheese*

Mix all together whilst potato and pumpkin are warm and serve.

# Sweet Pear Puree

**A recipe from Wendy Beattie who said "Pears are often referred to as a hypoallergenic fruit and are recommended as a safe way to start feeding your baby solids."**

- *1 pear*
- *1 tsp. brown sugar*

Peel pear and remove top. Sprinkle with brown sugar and bake for 3 minutes. Mash, cool and serve.

# Sweet Potato & Fruit Mash

**A favourite in Kim's household.**

- *1 green apple, peeled and chopped*
- *200g sweet potato, peeled and chopped*
- *6 plump blueberries*

Place apple and sweet potato in a saucepan with 375ml water and boil until tender. Add blueberries and puree, serve warm.

*Optional: Add corn from a corn on the cob, that has also been boiled, to the mix before pureeing.*


# Vegieblend

- *1 cup pumpkin (or sweet potato)*
- *1 cup carrot*
- *1 cup broccoli*

Steam all vegetables then either mash or blend well with ¼ cup of breast milk or pasteurized only milk.


*And LOTS and LOTS*
*of fresh fruit*
*and raw vegie sticks,*
*start them early*
*on the good stuff!*

# For The Pet

*We can judge the heart of a man by his treatment of animals.*

Immanual Kant

## Birdie Breakfast Cereal

- *¼ cup (25g) oats*
- *1 tsp. peanut butter*
- *¼ cup chopped apples or oranges*

Place oats in a microwave safe dish, cover with water and microwave on high for 1 minute. Remove the bowl, stir until the water is absorbed and the oatmeal is soft and cooked through. Add peanut butter and stir until dissolved. Stir in the fruit, allow to cool, stir and serve.

## Bird Sandwich

- *1 slice wholegrain bread*
- *1 jar fruit baby food*
- *½ cup chopped fruit or nuts*

Spread baby food on wholemeal bread and add chopped fruit, vegetables or nuts.

*Optional: Substitute fruit for jar of vegetable baby food and ½ cup chopped vegies for fruit.*

# Kitty Delight

- *1 cup (185g) white rice*
- *200g can tuna*
- *½ cup (125ml) milk*
- *1 can wet cat food*

Cook the white rice until soft, add all other ingredients and stir until well blended.


# Mini Morsels for Mature Cats

- *120g can sardines, packed in olive oil*
- *1 cup (130g) wholegrain bread crumbs*
- *1 free range egg, beaten*

Preheat oven to 150°C. Pour contents of sardines in a medium bowl. Using a fork, mash into tiny pieces. Add remaining ingredients and mix well. Drop ¼ tsp. of mixture onto a paper lined baking tray and bake in oven for 7 minutes. Store in airtight container.


# Dog Biscuits

- *250g liver*
- *2½ cups (440g) plain flour*
- *2½ cups (440g) wheat meal*
- *1 cup (130g) bran*

Preheat oven to 200°C. Place liver in a saucepan and cover with water, bring to the boil. Mince it and add remaining ingredients, mix well. Roll out and cut into thick slices. Bake for 10 minutes.

# Mint Rice Hamburgers

- 5 cups (925g) uncooked rice
- 10 cups (2.5 ltr.) water
- 1 kg lean hamburger mince
- 5 tbs. dried mint

Place rice and water in a large saucepan, bring to the boil. Add hamburger mince and mint and bring back to boil. Mix well. Reduce heat to low and simmer until all the water is absorbed. This is a great dinner for doggy halitosis!

# Fish Food

- 2cm x 2cm piece of pumpkin

A small seeded, peeled piece of pumpkin dropped into a fish tank will delight fish. It floats and takes about three days to eat.

# Fish Frankfurters

- ¼ Frankfurter, finely chopped

Ensure very small pieces so as to avoid your fish choking. Place small amount in fish tank and freeze the remaining.

# Leftover Ideas

*These are all fabulous ideas! But you should be aware that it takes energy to run large fridges and freezers so the first solution to utilise leftovers and minimise waste, should always be to shop to a menu and only buy what you are going to use!*

Many Thanks to Carolyn Markham of Bondi, NSW who inspired this section.

---

## Leftover Chicken Ideas

**Chicken & broccoli casserole for one:** ½ kg fresh or frozen broccoli, 1 cup shredded leftover chicken, ½ cup cream of chicken soup, ¼ cup grated parmesan cheese. Preheat oven to 180°C. Cook broccoli in boiling salted water. Drain. Grease a small casserole dish, place broccoli over bottom, top with chicken, pour over soup and sprinkle with parmesan. Bake for 10–15 minutes or until lightly browned and bubbling.

*Optional: Add ¼ tsp. cayenne pepper to soup.*

**Chicken & egg drop soup:** Heat one cup of water (250ml) to boiling on the stove, add 1 chicken stock cube, stir to dissolve. Take 1 egg and whisk it in a separate bowl. Using the whisk again, gently stream the egg into the boiling broth, reduce heat and gently stir. Add leftover shredded chicken and a vegie or two, simmer until ready.

**Chicken stir fry:** 1 cup shredded leftover chicken, 1 tbs. sesame oil, 3 tbs. your favourite bbq sauce. Heat oil in wok until hot, add sauce and mix until combined. Add chicken. Lower heat and cook until almost done (add more sauce if you like). Add vegetables and stir to cook for 3 minutes or to desired tenderness.

*Optional: You can make this vegetarian by omitting the chicken and adding tofu, nuts or even more vegies.*

---

**Chicken tacos or burritos:** Shred leftover chicken and 1–2 tsp. of your favourite bbq sauce, chill until sauce is completely absorbed in the chicken. Then make your own tacos or burritos with whatever salad your children will eat!

*Optional: Works just as nicely with left over mince.*

**Shred leftover chicken:** And mix with mayo, chopped tomato and fresh basil for a great sandwich filling.

# Leftover Fish Ideas

**Chop leftover tuna/fish cakes:** And mix with a dollop of mayonnaise. Place in a wrap for lunch and top with freshly shredded lettuce leaves.

**Cook salmon or prawns:** Can easily be turned into fishcakes by mixing with mashed potato, mayo and fresh herbs. Pan fry until crisp and serve with a dollop of Aioli (see Sauces).

**Fish:** Make a seafood sauce to have with pasta or rice.

**Fish toasties:** Flake leftover fish on top of toast. Top with cheese and grill. Cut into fingers and serve warm ... *Great for the kids!!*

**Fish cakes:** To leftover fish simply add mashed potato and an egg and mix well. Flavour with your choice of fresh herbs and spices, roll in breadcrumbs and bake or fry.

**Optional:** Serve with an easy dipping sauce made by combining equal parts of sweet chilli sauce and sour cream (add coriander if avaliable).

# Leftover Meat Ideas

**Dice the ham:** Add cold cooked green peas, cubed cheddar cheese and season with sea salt and pepper. Mix together with a bit of mayo.

*Optional: Add a little diced onion.*

**Ham bone:** Is very useful in adding flavour and thickening a pot of ham and pea or ham and bean soup.

**Leftover curries, sauces, soups:** Can be frozen — even if it's only enough for one portion, it's a solution for nights when you're home alone (and cheaper than takeaway!)

**Leftover roast pork:** Finely slice and stir fry pork with garlic, ginger, snow peas, roasted peanuts and soy sauce.

**Lunch:** Have a slice of ham on crunchy bread with Swiss cheese and seeded mustard.

**Meatloaf:** Spread fruit chutney and grated cheese over leftover meatloaf, then wrap in a sheet of ready rolled puff pastry before baking in the oven ... *Scrummy!*

**Ham mix:** Chopped green pepper and onions with cheese for a nice omelette.

**Stir fry beef mince:** With paprika, then add a can of tomatoes and kidney beans for a Mexican tortilla or nachos topping.

**Mince:** To ½ kg of mince add 1 packet of taco seasoning and shape into meatballs. Pour 2 tbs. olive oil into a frying pan and heat, brown meatballs, drain and serve in pita bread or burrito with salad and salsa.

# Leftover Rice Ideas

**Rice cakes:** Add 1 egg and ½ cup fresh breadcrumbs to leftover rice. Form into cakes and fry in extra virgin olive oil until nice and golden.

**Risotto balls:** Roll tbs. of leftover rice or risotto into balls. Push a small cube of mozzarella into the centre and roll in breadcrumbs. Bake in a moderate oven for 10–15 mins. Balls can be shallow fried if you are in a hurry.

*Hint: In all the rice recipes, use moistened hands so that the rice doesn't stick.*

**Surplus cooked rice:** Cook with chopped vegetables, cashews, eggs or diced bacon. Add some soya sauce and you have a yummy fried rice.

**Optional:** Also nice with a squirt of sweet chilli sauce.

**Stuffed peppers:** Leftover risotto, or other grain-based dishes like couscous can become a base for stuffed peppers. Just add your favourite freshly chopped herb to it prior to baking.

**To cold rice add:** Grated lemon and parsley, parmesan and nutmeg or chopped olives and lemon rind. Roll into little balls, dip in seasoned flour and beaten egg and roll in fresh breadcrumbs. Gently fry in oil until crisp and golden. Drain.

# Leftover Vegetable Ideas

**Add leftover vegies:** To risotto, chop roughly and stir through at the end of cooking with grated cheese.

**Baked potato toppings:** Chop leftovers finely, add them to baked potato and top with sour cream and cheese.

**Beetroot:** Place contents of opened canned beetroot in an airtight container and fill with a mixture of water and white vinegar. Refrigerate until needed, this helps keep beetroot fresh.

**Bubble and squeak:** Mash leftover vegies, mix with a dollop of leftover gravy or tomato sauce and fry in lots of hot oil.

**Fresh herbs:** Can be frozen if not used in time - defrosted, they're still OK in cooked dishes.

**Fritters:** Kim and Rachael's Mums have been making these for years! Perfect your classic fritter batter; 1¾ cups self raising flour, 1 cup milk, 1 egg, salt 'n' pepper … mix to quite a stiff batter and add to it whatever you want. Fry in lots of hot oil when ready.

**Optional:** For a variation, and if in your cupboard, season with a pinch of curry powder or Tabasco sauce etc.

**Grilled leftover vegies:** Arrange leftover vegetables in one layer in an ovenproof dish. Cover with 3–4 slices of Gruyere cheese and grill until cheese has melted and vegies are warm.

**Mashed for baby:** Mashing leftover vegies makes an ideal dish for baby's dinner.

**Peppers:** That are showing their age are shoved whole into the oven to roast, they are delicious in dips (see Red Yoghurt Dip) and soups (see Chorizo and Red Pepper Soup) … *Yum Scrum!*

**Potato crisps:** To crisp up leftover potato crisps, wrap them in a single layer of kitchen paper towel and microwave on high for 30 seconds.

**Tasty mashed potatoes:** Spoon leftovers into a dish, top with cheese, chopped bacon and paprika. Bake at 200°C for 10–12 minutes.

**Vegetable based dips:** eg., hummus can be divided into portions so half can be frozen if they won't be consumed quickly.

**Wilted vegetables:** Inevitably gather on the bottom of the fridge but can make a great soup with some leftover pasta and stock thrown in!

# Other Leftover Ideas

**Bread crusts:** Use leftover crusts by dipping them in melted butter, coating with finely grated cheese, then lightly sprinkling with curry powder. Cook in 200°C oven, until crisp and browned. Great served with dips.

**Fruitcake:** Use leftover fruitcake in rum balls (*4 Ingredients*) and stuffed, baked apples (*4 Ingredients 2.*)

**Leftover fruit:** Anything wrinkling or over ripe becomes stewed fruit to eat with yoghurt, muesli or stirred into porridge — except for bananas, mangoes or strawberries which are frozen for later use in baking.

**Plum pudding:** Fry slices of plum pudding in a little unsalted butter for 2 minutes on each side. Serve warm with custard or ice cream.

**Stale cereals and nuts:** Pop them on a plate and microwave on high for 40 seconds. Then set aside to cool and crisp up.

**Leftover liquid from canned fruit:** Boil it until it's reduced by half. Add seasoning and use it to baste chicken. It tastes delicious and will keep the chicken moist.

**Left over wine:** Freeze wine into ice cube trays and use in cooking.

**Spaghetti Bolognaise:** On a sheet of ready rolled puff pastry, spread bolognaise leaving a 2cm border. Top with baby spinach and grated parmesan cheese. Roll up the sheet and glaze with a beaten egg. Place on a paper lined baking tray and bake in at 200°C oven for 20 minutes or until golden.

# Making More Time For You!

By Rachael Bermingham

If there's one thing I know something about it's about how to fit in all the things I want to do into a single day. It hasn't always been the case though, and I must say, it never came naturally: In fact many years ago I had to learn it and let me tell you it was quite easily one of the most challenging things I ever did — but also one of the most beneficial too!

Fortunately I persisted, as it's been invaluable in enabling me to do everything I've wanted to do. In the past 3 years I've managed to run 2 businesses solo and co run 2 others from my home office during my gorgeous little boy Jaxson's sleep time. For 1½ years of that time (while I co wrote 2 books) my husband worked away on shifts ranging from 5 days on 4 off, to 11 days on 3 off. As a result whenever I am speaking at a seminar, people always ask 'How do you fit it all in?' After all it doesn't matter who you are, what your family circumstances are, we are ALL busy. It's just working out how to maximise that 24 hour period so it works for you rather than against you.

Here's my top tips on making more time for YOU, from one busy person to another. I hope they are as helpful to you as they have been to me so you can spend more time for YOU!!

**1. GET A DIARY OR SCHEDULE**. This is not only a FANTASTIC resource for managing your time, but it also helps you to remember everything important and allows you to see what you have in your day already so you don't over commit.

**2. PLAN.** I believe this is the single most important part in achieving anything and for clawing back some much needed YOU time. Spend some time planning what you want to do so you know what steps you need to take and when. This assists you in making relevant choices that move you closer to your goals.

**3. PRIORITISE.** Work out what is important to you and ensure you allocate plenty of time for those things first. For example my husband and son are my very first priority. So everything to do with them I schedule in first, friends come a very close second followed by business, then me and then the household. This may be different for you so you simply need to schedule according to what you see as important in your life.

**4. BE RUTHLESS.** I was always what I call a YES person. Whenever someone asked me to do something I'd say 'YES!' Howeeevvveerrrrrr this always left me highly over committed and usually stressed! My diary is a great tool for helping me to be ruthless with my time. When someone asks if I can do something I say 'sure, let me check my schedule' and I'll see where I can slot the activity in. If it's next week or in 5 months time I am comfortable about responding and KNOW that if my 24 hours is booked up then it's booked up – if you work with it, it makes life a whole lot easier.

**5. OUTSOURCING WHAT YOU PROCRASTINATE ON.** We've all got our strengths (and just quietly, our weaknesses too). My weakness is in MYOB data entry. I know it rings some people's bells, but not mine. I wasn't blessed with administrative talent for it. It's not that I can't do it – I simply don't enjoy doing it. I know, without a shadow of doubt, that if left up to me, everything would wait until the last possible date when I would then find myself working like a mad woman to get it all updated in time. So to alleviate any stress or costly mistakes, I have a bookkeeper who is simply sensational and LOVES, LOVES, LOVES doing it and does it incredibly well. I'm happy, she's happy and the tax man is happy so everyone wins and we're all doing the things we love rather than stressing over what we don't.

**6. MINIMISE UNECESSARY TASKS.** Before I did get organised, one thing you would find me doing CONSTANTLY was going to the supermarket every other day to get ingredients for dinner. Often it would be a costly trip. 1/ because I'd go in without really thinking what we were having for dinner so would end up with a variety of ingredients I didn't even get to use, and 2/ because I was wasting time and fuel in doing it! So if you can plan your weekly shopping menu and add all the required ingredients to your list then you won't have to visit the supermarket more than once a week, you save time travelling back and forth AND you save money too! Happy Days!!!

**7. USE COMPUTER TIME EFFECTIVELY.** We've probably all been guilty of a little out of school internet surfing right? But it's one of THE biggest time zappers around. One site leads into another and another etc, before you know it 2 hours has slipped away from you. The other time zapper is emails. If you find yourself checking emails every 10 minutes or whiling away the hours in cyberspace, then a great tip I utilise is to allocate time for computer research and also emails. I book a block of time for research and also check emails 3 times throughout the day; first thing in the morning, after lunch when Jaxson is sleeping and again when he goes to sleep at night and only on my work days, never on my days off. This was really challenging to get used to, but it's sensational when you get the hang of it. You can fit in far more to your day.

**8. ALLOCATE A BUFFER ZONE.** We all have unexpected things that come up. Friends pop in, someone needs you to help them urgently, a job takes a little longer, transport is delayed, you slept in, or sometimes you just didn't feel like doing something that you had to do (which often masquerades the fact that you need to take a little time out!) ... Each day wherever possible, make a space in your diary for a buffer zone so you still have another block of time to have another crack at finishing something. AND if you have finished everything, then you can relax and spend that time on YOU! Wooooo hoooo!

Remember what we focus on is forever changing so you need to be flexible and be prepared to allow for changes to your lifestyle (like babies, retirement). Under-commit rather than over-commit every chance you get so you can stop and smell the roses. We've all got 24 hours in the day, so make the most of yours every moment you get!

# Budget Menu Ideas

There are plenty of recipes from within the pages of *4 Ingredients 2* that will help you impress any gathering on any occasion.

Here are a couple of examples, that people just like you suggested!!!

# Date Night Menu

*"You must be the change you wish to see in the world."*

Mahatma Ghandi

---

### NIBBLES

Feta Dip

*Served with: Melba toast & fresh, julienned vegetables*

### ENTRÉE

Tomato Soup

*Served with: Fresh crusty bread*

### MAIN

Veal & Pesto Rolls

*Served with: Mashed Potato, Herbed Zucchini*

### DESSERT

Baked Apples with a Twist

# Girls Luncheon Menu

*"My boyfriend used to ask his mother,*
*'How can I find the right woman for me?' and she would answer,*
*'Don't worry about finding the right woman,*
*concentrate on becoming the right man.'"*

Unknown

---

### NIBBLES

Asparagus Wraps
& Baked Haloumi

### MAIN

Balsamic Glazed Lamb Cutlets

*Served with: Feta & Watermelon Salad*

### DESSERT

Toblerone Dip

*Served with: A mezze of fresh, sliced fruit*

### DRINKS

Mint Tea or
A glass of Bubbles

# Vegetarian Dinner Party Menu

*"Nothing will benefit human health and increase the chances for survival of life on Earth as much as the evolution to a vegetarian diet."*

Albert Einstein

---

## NIBBLES

Warm Cheese Dip

*Served with: Slices of fresh, crusty bread & a mezze of fresh vegetables*

## ENTRÉE

Tempting Mini-Pizzas

## MAIN

Baked Ricotta Pie

*Served with: Green salad drizzled with a delicious Balsamic Dressing*

## DESSERT

Frozen Yoghurt Tarts

# A Bachelor's Guide to Dinner

*A computer once beat me at chess, but it was no match for me at kick boxing !!!!!*

Emo Philips

---

## NIBBLES

Easy Pork Bites

## MAIN

Bbq Beef Stir Fry

*Served with: Boiled Rice*

## DESSERT

Little Lemon Cheesecakes

# Kid's Party Ideas

*We worry about what a child will become tomorrow, yet we forget that he is someone today.*

Stacia Tauscher

---

### NIBBLES

Fruit Kebabs

Date Slice

Pikelets

### LUNCH

Chicken Carnival Cones

Sausage Rolls

Mini Cheese Quiches

### DESSERT

Caramel, Choc Truffles

Jelly in Oranges

Birthday Cake

### DRINKS

Water

*Served with: Ice-cubes that have been frozen with drop of food colouring in them.*

*You can make different colours for a pretty rainbow effect!*

# Notes

# Notes

# Biographies

## Kim McCosker

Kim was born in Stanthorpe but raised in Mundubbera, Queensland. Schooled on the Gold Coast, Kim attended Star of the Sea Catholic High School and Griffith University, completing a Bachelor of International Finance. Kim trained with MLC as a Financial Planner, completing her Diploma in Financial Planning through Deakin University in 2000. Kim's natural ease with people, her ability to communicate effortlessly and her country confidence served her extremely well as a successful financial adviser and later as the Queensland State Manager of MLC Private Client Services. After the birth of her second child, Kim resigned and worded from home contract writing financial plans.

It was during this phase of her life that *4 Ingredients* was brought to life. Kim had the bright idea, but it was at the suggestion of her life-long friend Rachael Bermingham that they write the book ... And so over a couple of red wines began the wonderful rollercoaster ride *4 Ingredients* would go on to become! Taking a year to compile and cook, *4 Ingredients* (or Kim's fourth child as she lovingly refers to it) was launched on the 14th March 2007. From an initial print run of 2,000 that was deemed "over-ambitious in a market saturated with cookbooks" Kim and Rachael went on to orchestrate what the book trade now refers to as "an absolute phenomenon" having written a book that ended 2007 as one of the biggest selling books, across all genres, in both Australia and New Zealand.

And as Kim says "No-one was more surprised than us!".

In addition to this, over the past 8 years, Glen and Kim have bought and renovated several properties, including a 1957 Anglican Church, a beachside shack, and the current house they now live in on the Sunshine Coast's beautiful Pelican Waters. Without a sliver of doubt however, the most rewarding of everything accomplished to date has been the birth of her three precious little boys Morgan 8, Hamilton 5 and Flynn, 2. For Kim, family is THE MOST IMPORTANT and carries the greatest priority of all she does! Renovations to properties were done with the children playing in the yard, recipes tested with them mixing and stirring, books written around their sleep times and trips made only when her wonderfully supportive and much loved husband Glen could be home for them.

Life presents many opportunities, but having the courage to pursue them, in what is an ever increasingly busy and demanding world, is hard. But Kim is living proof that you can achieve whatever you want in life with exactly that ... Hard work!

You can contact Kim by email: **Kim@4ingredients.com.au**

Or by snail mail: **PO Box 1171 Mooloolaba QLD Australia 4557.**

# Rachael Bermingham

Rachael Bermingham (nee Moore) was born in Stanthorpe before moving to the Sunshine Coast at 11 where she grew up and still resides with husband Paul (a renovator) and gorgeous sons Jaxson, 5 and twins Bowie and Casey, 2 months old. She is also 'wicked' step mum to Lee 19 and Teri 17.

Working from her home office, Rachael co-runs *4 Ingredients* and Sunshine Coast Speakers and solo operates her personal speaking engagements and *Read My Lips*: her 1st self published book she co-wrote to inspire women to achieve their goals (first published 14/2/06) which she penned out while feeding baby Jaxson.

A born entrepreneur Rachael showed her keen eye for business early on with the launch of her first business venture (the first mobile hair salon on the Sunshine Coast) at age 19 that she built up for a year, and sold for a profit before going onto experience a host of bold careers to satisfy her adventurous nature, including diving and shark feeding at Underwater World before her passion for business returned in the form of travel.

After a 5 year stint as a Flight Centre travel agent, Rachael entered into what could have been considered a fatal business move by opening her own travel agency just 3 months prior to September 11. This experience would ultimately prove to be a pivotal point in her career igniting the development of an ability which would be invaluable for Rachael, *Read My Lips* and *4 Ingredients* and inspire others in business around the world as well.

With the travel trade in a spin, Rachael didn't give up; instead she worked well into the early morning hours teaching herself how to market so her business would survive in the industry's most ruinous era. Researching and testing LOTS and LOTS (and LOTS!) of strategies, she learnt the art of marketing and found she LOVED it and thankfully had a real knack for it.

Her talent for marketing and publicity soon became well known and requests from others to help them also started coming in. She sat on various business boards including an RSL, town developmental board and a business women's board before leaving travel to take on the first of many businesses she would build from a tiny turnover to an astonishing MULTI MILLION dollar turnovers within months AND without spending a cent on advertising! Right up to an hour of going into labour, Rachael was still actively involved in mentoring and helping business owners in 6 different countries.

Within days of becoming a Mum, Rachael known for her abundant energy and enthusiasm continued to pursue her passion for business instigating a motivational seminar for women encompassing life, health, wealth and business success strategies with the help of some of girlfriends that ran for 2 years and morphed into the book *Read My Lips*.

It was by giving Read My Lips to Kim as a gift at Jaxsons 1st birthday party that would prove to be the beginning of yet another incredible journey for Rachael. Prompted by Rachael's passing comment of "They say everyone has a good book in them" Kim entrusted her own fabulous idea for a book with Rachael (a cookbook using a few ingredients) which Rachael immediately loved and proceeded to prod Kim to start compiling (mainly so Rachael herself could use it!!!) Kim after a few weeks said that she'd do it on the condition "that you write it with me!" And the rest is beautiful history!

These days when Rachael's not enjoying time with her family, cooking up a storm with Kim, or working on other books, she loves speaking at conferences to inspire others to achieve their own goals. She also enjoys talking on time management, life balance, how to develop a business from home and of course marketing and publicity.

You can contact Rachael by email: **Rachael@4ingredients.com.au**

Or by snail mail: **PO Box 1171 Mooloolaba QLD Australia 4557.**

# Bibliography

## Books

Cyndi O'Meara. **Changing Habits Changing Lives**. Penguin Books Victoria, Australia 2000.

Cyndi O'Meara. **Changing Habits Changing Lives Cookbook**. Penguin Books Victoria, Australia 2002.

Kim Morrison and Fleur Welligan. **Like Chocolate for Women**. Random House. Auckland, New Zealand 2004.

Kim Morrison and Fleur Welligan. **About Face**. Random House. Auckland, New Zealand 2007.

Nestle. **Sweet Treats – 50 Family Favourites**. FPC Living (Books Division) General Newspapers Pty Ltd, 2002.

Culinary Arts Institute. **Encyclopaedic Cookbook**. Book Production Industries, Inc. Chicago, Illinois, 1959.

Bay Books. **Mother's Favourite Recipes – the Best of Traditional Home Cooking**. Bay Books 61-69 Anzac Parade, Kensington NSW 2033, 1985.

Margaret Fulton. **Encyclopaedia of Food & Cookery**. Octopus Pty Ltd. 44 Market Street, Sydney, NSW 2000, 1983.

**The Presbyterian Cookery Book**. Compiled for The Women's Missionary Association of the Presbyterian Church of New South Wales. 1950.

Anne Marshall. **Anne's Perfect Piebook**. Paul Hamlyn Pty Ltd. 176 South Creek Road, Dee Why West New South Wales 2099. 1979.

**Small Food**. Murdoch Books. GPO Box 1203 Sydney, New South Wales 1045. 2002.

A Parragon Book. **Perfect Tapas**. Parragon 4 Queens Street Bath BA1 1HE, UK. 2007.

Anne Thorpe. **The Australian Cookbook**. Child & Henry Publishing P/L 9 Clearview Place, Brookvale, NSW 2100.

Gabrielle Bluett. **50 Easy Low Salt Recipes**. Self-published. 8/46 Muston Street, Mosman NSW 2088.

# Webpages

### Winter Fruits – April – December
www.aumann.com.au/fruit-winter.htm

### Baby Food
www.essentialbaby.com.au/page/essential_recipes.html
www.wholesomebabyfood.com/baby-food-freezing-chart.htm

### "Leftover Rescue Tips" December 2003
www.recipezaar.com

### "What to do with leftover chicken dishes"
www.leftoverchicken.com/recipes/view_recipe.php?recipeid=26

### "Remains of the day: why eating leftovers can save the planet."
blogs.smh.com.au/lifestyle/chewonthis/archives/2007/11/remains_of_the_day_eat_leftove.html

### "Footprints: Tread lightly into the future.
www.northsydney.nsw.gov.au/footprints/resources_cleaning.asp

### Poems for Parents
home.att.net/~DLeddy/ppoems.html

### Laurent Caters for Kids
www.laurentcaters.com.au

### Read My Lips
www.readmylips.com

# Index

## If a Child Lives with Criticism ............................... **189**

## FOR THE CHILDREN.......................................... **190**

## Savoury............................................................ **190**

## Sweet................................................................ **200**

# Invitation

To all who contributed a recipe to this book, by way of email, post or phone, we would like to extend *a sincere* thank you.

IF YOU have a fabulous 4 or 5 ingredient recipe and think that others would enjoy cooking it please submit it at **www.4ingredients.co.uk**

Be sure to include your name, suburb or town for acknowledgment.

## *Thank You*

## *Best Wishes & Happy Cooking!*

*Rachael & Kim*

4

*Ingredients*

2